LEADERSHIP

ON THE AXIS OF CHANGE

CHICK YUILL

CREST BOOKS

The Salvation Army National Publications
Alexandria, Virginia

Published by Crest Books, Salvation Army National Headquarters
615 Slaters Lane, Alexandria, Virginia 22314
(703) 299–5558 Fax: (703) 684–5539
http://www.salvationarmyusa.org

Printed in the United States of America

Cover design by Laura Ezzell
Composition by Jennifer Williams

Library of Congress Control Number: 2003111210

ISBN: 0–9740940–0–5

Leadership on the Axis of Change

This book is dedicated to

_____

All those who have been my leaders;
All those who have accepted me as their leader;
And—above all—to the Great Leader
Whose service and sacrifice provide us with the perfect model.

Contents

introduction

Calling All Leaders

**And if the man who plays the bugle does not sound a clear call,
who will prepare for the battle?**

1 Corinthians 14:8, Good News Bible

Leadership is not a quality reserved for presidents and prime ministers, for those in the upper echelons of business or with high-profile ministries in the church. Leadership is needed in all sectors of society and at every level of human endeavor. We are indeed grateful for the examples of those in business, government, and the church who have massive leadership gifts, whose names appear in our bookshops and who are known and respected throughout the world. But all too often we can be discouraged by these "heavyweights" of leadership. Their exceptional personalities and their outstanding gifts and abilities can be intimidating, and they can blind us to the fact that many of us are called to lead.

Leading by Example

Some have the gift of leadership in greater measure than others. But many more have the potential for leadership than we often recognize. More than a few examples are found in the Bible of seemingly unlikely people who are called by God to a life of leadership. Consider Moses. He fled from Egypt as a fugitive from Pharaoh after he had come to the defense of a Hebrew slave by murdering an abusive Egyptian commandant. Egypt was the last place Moses would have chosen to return—especially if it involved a face-to-face encounter with Pharaoh! So when God spoke to him out of the burning bush, the words must have struck terror in Moses' heart:

> I have indeed seen the misery of My people in Egypt. . . . So now, go. I am sending you to Pharaoh to bring My people the Israelites out of Egypt. (Exodus 3:7–10)

Little wonder that Moses offered a list of excuses. Who was he to go to Pharaoh? What would he tell people about his encounter with God? Who, if anyone, would believe him? Surely God was aware that Moses was no speaker, that he stumbled over his words. When God answered Moses' every objection with the promise of His power and presence, Moses resorted to the plea which thousands have echoed through the centuries: "O Lord, please send someone else to do it" (Exodus 4:13). Little wonder that even the Creator of the universe began to get angry! In the end, however, Moses answered the call, and although he still had much to learn, history shows him to be one of the great leaders of the ages.

Few of us will hear God's voice from a burning bush; few of us will be called to face the awesome political power of a despotic ruler; few of us will be entrusted with the destiny of an entire nation. But many of us will be called by God to exercise leadership that will have serious consequences in time and eternity. Like Moses, we will have much to learn, and our latent abilities will need to be developed by training and practice in the art of leadership. But we must first, like Moses, answer the call.

If we open our eyes and minds, we can see positive examples of leadership right in front of us. In the week I am writing this chapter, my colleague Ivor is about to take a team to Afghanistan to set up a short-term refugee program. He has no blueprint to follow. An unavoidable element of risk is involved in the project, and he will be separated from his family for six weeks. But he is as excited and happy as I have ever seen him. Why? Because he loves to lead. He is busy setting up the team, tying up loose ends, and making sure that everything will move forward swiftly and efficiently. All over the world there are people like Ivor getting other people to do things that will demonstrate God's love and change the world for the better. Whether they call themselves leaders or not, they are leaders; and if reading about Ivor's plans sets your pulse racing just a bit and gives you even the slightest twinge of envy, then leadership may be your gift more than you realize—and this book may be of some use in helping you develop that gift to its fullest potential.

Leadership is not an exclusive talent belonging to the favored few. It is a desperate need—belonging in our churches and communities. The church in the twenty-first century faces great challenges stemming from inert cynicism within and dynamic change without. Leaders are needed to answer the fundamental questions of *identity* and *membership*: Who are we and what is our mission? How do we encourage people to belong in a post-denominational, postmodern world in which they are not naturally "joiners"? The church needs men and women who will do the hard thinking and make the bold decisions that will drive forward change.

Answering the Call

The great Swiss psychiatrist Carl Gustav Jung said that "the true leader is always led." His words ring with challenge and comfort for everyone called to spiritual leadership, for we are all followers of the greatest leader who ever lived. Of course, we will never equal Jesus in the quality of our leadership any more than we will do so in the quality of our lives. But that does not alter the fact that we have before us the perfect example of leadership, an example that we will examine in a later chapter.

Within the Body of Christ, leadership is more than merely a human quality. It is a spiritual gift.

> We have different gifts according to the grace given us. . . .
> If it is leadership, let him govern diligently. (Romans 12)

It is the role of the church or community to identify and equip those having the gift of leadership, and it is the role of the leader to accept the responsibility of exercising and developing this gift as God gives him or her opportunity. It is the disciplined work of a lifetime. And it is to helping those engaged in this lifelong task that this book is addressed.

one

A Changing World

A new civilization is emerging. . . .
This new civilization brings with it new family styles; changed ways
of working, loving and living. . . .
Millions are already tuning their lives to the rhythms of tomorrow. . . .
The dawn of this new civilization
is the single most explosive fact of our lifetimes.

Alvin Toffler, The Third Wave

Never in the history of humankind have people witnessed such rapid and discontinuous changes as are happening almost daily. Few would have predicted the collapse of communism, the rise of Islamic fundamentalism, the revival of ancient feuds, and the redrawing of the map in eastern Europe. Who could have foreseen the attack on the Twin Towers in New York City and the resulting impact on the psyche of the Western world? In addition to the unprecedented advances in technology and medicine, another change is taking place in our society—a shift that profoundly influences the culture in which the Christian Church must witness and serve. It is an inevitable change which calls for wise, discerning leadership.

The Third Wave

From the Age of Discovery through the Industrial Revolution, modernity—where reason reigns supreme—has been the prevailing philosophy for much of western culture. The church has struggled to engage in dialogue with that mindset for nearly five hundred years, seeking to demonstrate that religious faith is rational, applying the same analytical thinking to issues of biblical interpretation, morality, and the communication of the gospel. But now the church is again struggling to come to terms with a profound paradigm shift: Modernity has been overtaken by postmodernity.

The term *postmodernity* was first coined in the 1930s and was later used by the historian Arnold Toynbee to describe the culture and philosophy that began to emerge in Europe following World War I. It gained greater currency when used to describe movements and tendencies in art, literature, and architecture in the 1960s and 1970s. In the following decades its meaning grew to embrace an emerging worldview that permeated the arts, philosophy, politics, science, theology, and much of the popular culture. This new worldview was rooted in the fact that scientific and technological advances brought with them problems arguably greater than those they solved. Confronted with terrible threats of nuclear and biological warfare, horrors of pollution, and the possibility of our planet's extinction, it became all too apparent that human reason was unable to deliver what it had promised. Rationalistic materialism and faith in inevitable progress were seen as hollow shams.

Postmodernity is a slippery concept. It does, however, have some overriding characteristics, which, when clearly identified, confront today's leaders with an unescapable challenge: How would God have His Church respond effectively?

- Postmodernists see the universe not as a vast machine made from an infinite number of working parts, but rather as an organic, dynamic whole that can only be understood as part of a great cosmic process continually created and redefined. They willingly accept and enjoy the products of scientific progress, but they reject the mechanistic world-view that led to such progress.

- Postmodernists no longer trust in human reason. They reject the notion of an objective truth applicable to all people and for all time. Instead, if it works for you, then that's your truth.

- Postmodernists reject the idea of a mega–narrative, a big story that explains what life is all about, giving meaning and purpose to existence. Instead, each person creates their own meaning through their unique experiences.

If there is no absolute truth and no overarching story to define reality and provide a standard of behavior for all, then tolerance replaces truth as the great virtue. Indeed, right and wrong become almost entirely matters of personal opinion. It all depends on your point of view; how things appear depends on where you are standing. As Richard Rorty, the writer of *Contingency, Irony and Solidarity* (Cambridge University Press), put it: "Anything can be made to look good or bad by being redescribed." In a postmodern world, all lifestyles and all moral positions are equally valid.

Although postmodern culture rejects organized religion, it would be inaccurate to describe it as unspiritual. Indeed, its rejection of human reason as the ultimate arbiter of truth, its dismissal of the concept of a mechanistic universe, and its emphasis on individual experience mean that it is open to spirituality in a way that was never characteristic of modernity. But this spirituality is eclectic. It is a kind of spirituality with a smorgasbord mentality—mix and match and come up with whatever suits you. New Age religion, for example, with its combination of eastern religion, occult practices and pseudo–science, is a result of a postmodern mindset.

Even the concept of "self" is a matter of skepticism for the postmodern thinker. He sees a world where there is no ultimate meaning, no enduring relationships, just transient encounters and fleeting images. In an interview with *Newsweek* in 1997 Bob Dylan eloquently, if bleakly, expressed the experience of living in this changed world: "I don't think I'm tangible to myself. I mean, I think one thing today and I think another thing tomorrow. I change during the course of a day. I wake and I'm one person, and when I go to sleep I know for certain that I'm somebody else. I don't know who I am most of the time. It doesn't even matter to me."

In his book *Reality Isn't What It Used to Be*, Walter Truett Anderson uses the story about three baseball umpires to perfectly sum up the change from modernity to postmodernity:

> The first umpire said, "There's balls and there's strikes, and I call 'em the way they are."

> The second umpire said, "There's balls and there's strikes, and I call 'em the way I see 'em."

> The third umpire said, "There's balls and there's strikes, and they ain't nothin' until I call 'em!"

The first comment represents *modernity*—the assumption that human reason can observe and describe objective reality. The second comment is *humility*—the belief that there is an objective reality tempered by the recognition that human reason is frail and imperfect. The third comment is pure *postmodernity*—reality only exists and only has meaning insofar as it is within my experience.

Ramifications of a Postmodern Worldview

FROM CO-WORKER TO CONSUMER

Under an agricultural economy, we were co-workers. We shared the toil and shared the produce. The move to an industrial economy ushered in an age of consumerism, and the unprecedented results of mass production gave us the never-before-dreamed opportunity for mass consumption. When I would accompany my parents to the local grocery store as a child, basic food items were available and nothing more. Now, when I go shopping with my wife, I enter a supermarket with thousands of products on the shelves. When buying breakfast cereal, I am confronted with a bewildering variety of choices. The resulting mental paralysis of people like me, when faced with such decisions, has led to the latest stage in consumerism—customization. The message to the consumer today is, "We'll not only give you a choice—we'll package it to match your needs."

FROM PARAGRAPHS TO PICTURES

Every couple of months I spend a morning with Alastair, our youth work specialist, and together we compile a newsletter. I come up with the words and Alastair sets them out on the page, complete with appropriate clip art and other visual material. Alastair is certainly not in any way less articulate than I am. We simply divide the labor largely because of the difference in our ages; Alastair is twenty–five years younger. I grew up in a book culture. Consequently, I think sequentially—in a logical and linear way. Alastair is a child of a visual, consumer culture, having grown up in a world of rapidly changing, rapidly moving images—the world of MTV and the internet. Whereas I automatically structure my thinking in paragraphs, he much more naturally thinks in pictures. The variance in our approach—mine, systemic; his, organic—precisely reflects a key difference between modernity and postmodernity.

FROM ETHICS TO AESTHETICS

Postmodernity has not only rejected an external morality, it has also forsaken the search for an internal reality. The fragmentation of the self that Bob Dylan spoke of in his *Newsweek* interview makes such a quest futile and unproductive. Now the concern focuses on style, appearance, packaging. This is the age of cosmetic dentistry, plastic surgery, personal trainers, the pursuit of the perfect body and eternal youth, style gurus and the cult of celebrity, finding and expressing our worth and identity through the expensive brand names attached to the things we own. We have all been caught up, more than we would care to admit, in the journey from ethics to aesthetics.

FROM JOINERS TO JUGGLERS

In his significant work, *Bowling Alone* (Simon & Schuster), Robert Putnam states that far fewer Americans are joining organized groups or getting involved in civic life than once was the case. Service clubs, political parties, and churches are all affected. The wealth of facts and figures and the pages of scholarly analysis in his book leave the reader with no doubt that his observations are accurate.

Putnam states that the generations born after World War II do not join organizations to the same extent that their parents and grandparents did, and he suggests a number of reasons for this trend: financial and time pressures, particularly on two–career families; suburbanization and commuting; and electronic entertainment (particularly television) that absorbs our free time. Instead, these postmodernists will join groups for their own purposes and to suit their ever–changing priorities. They are jugglers rather than joiners. The typical two–career family has numerous plates to keep spinning: jobs, advanced academic studies, family commitments, networks of friends and acquaintances, children's education. They are more likely to find time to join the local health or golf club and to support the local football team than to commit themselves to a long–term membership in a church or Rotary club.

FROM PRINCIPLES TO PEOPLE

I love the story of Eric Liddell, my fellow Scotsman, whose life has been immortalized in the movie *Chariots of Fire*. Liddell refused to run in the hundred–meter race at the Paris Olympics in 1924, even though he was the favorite for the gold medal. His refusal was based solely on the fact that it was against his principles to run on a Sunday.

Few people know the sequel to the part of Liddell's life depicted in the film. He later went to China as a missionary and was interred as a prisoner of war during World War I. One Sunday some of the young people in the prison camp went out to play field hockey and asked Liddell to referee their game. As he had done at the Olympics, Liddell refused: "I don't play games on the Lord's Day," he explained. Predictably, without a referee, the game ended in a fight. The next Sunday, when the youngsters went out to play again, the man who would not deny his principles for Olympic gold chose to put people before principles and became their referee.

Liddell was a man of conservative values, but on that day he was acting more like postmodern man. It often seems that in today's world there are no moral values at all. To a large extent, that criticism is valid. But if you scratch the surface, you will find a kind of selective morality that places people before principles. It is undeniable that traditional moral values have been abandoned by many. Marriage, for example, is seen as just one lifestyle choice among others. Yet some aspects of the postmodern moral code are stricter than those held by previous generations. The days when a male boss could make sexually suggestive remarks to a female employee and pass it off as just workplace banter are long gone. The physical and sexual abuse of children is deplored and exposed as never before. Individual rights are prized and protected more than at any previous time.

Issachar Leaders

All too often the Christian Church is seen as the last bastion of conservatism—suspicious of and resistant to any kind of change. Like Mark Twain, we cry, "I'm all for progress; it's change I don't like." But we live in a changing world. What's more, God has brought His church into existence to be the supreme agent of change. Its mission is not to stop the future but to shape it. The whole creation, as Paul points out in the eighth chapter of the Letter to the Romans, is looking to the people of God and longing for the ultimate purpose and pattern of God to be demonstrated in a confused world:

> The creation waits in eager expectation for the sons of God
> to be revealed. For the creation was subjected to frustration,
> not by its own choice, but by the will of the one who sub-
> jected it, in hope that the creation itself will be liberated from
> its bondage to decay and brought into the glorious freedom
> of the children of God.

Therefore, Christian leaders in the twenty-first century need to be leaders of change. And unless the church and its leaders consider the post-modern worldview far more seriously than we have done up to this point, we are doomed to fail in our God-given calling to transform and challenge the people. (This point is further addressed in a later chapter.)

A telling passage is found in the twelfth chapter of 1 Chronicles, where the ancient historian of Israel listed all the tribes who rallied to King David in battle when he led the nation of Israel against them. Each tribe brought thousands of men armed for battle, except for the tribe of Issachar, which sent only two hundred chiefs with their relatives. They, however, proved to be invaluable. The chronicler describes them simply as "men of Issachar, who understood the times and knew what Israel should do."

We need such men and women today—Issachar leaders who hold the newspaper in one hand and the Bible in the other, informed leaders who understand the significant movements in our society, intelligent leaders who thoughtfully consider both the culture in which we live and the creed by which we live. We need those who are willing to lead the people of God in the kind of action that will bring about the answer to the prayer that Jesus taught those first leaders of His church to utter—the ultimate change for which the entire creation is longing:

> Our Father in heaven, hallowed be Your name, Your kingdom come, Your will be done on earth as it is in heaven. (Matthew 6:9,10)

two

A Dying Church

The present cultural upheaval from modernity to postmodernity . . . will necessitate not merely the structural re–engineering of denominations but their death and resurrection.

Eddie Gibbs, Church Next

The Salvation Army was born in the Industrial world of Victorian England. It was a world of slow and gradual change, a world that suited the hierarchical, quasi–military structure that William Booth adopted for his newly formed movement. But Booth was the ultimate pragmatist, the man who was later to say that he began with a blank sheet of paper and borrowed ideas from everywhere, doggedly retaining those that worked and readily discarding those that failed.

As we face a very different world—a world marked by pluralism, secularism, and rapid, discontinuous change—we need to recover the same pragmatism, ruggedly holding to the mission with which we have been entrusted but willingly abandoning whatever precludes that mission. If we are to talk seriously about the kind of leaders we need for the age in which

13

we live, we cannot avoid facing the challenge of the kind of church we need to be in order to serve the present age and fulfill our calling. A changed world can only be reached by a changed church.

Safety to Sacrifice

One thing is clear—the status quo is not an option. For anyone who tries to engage with the world outside the church, there can be no doubt that Europe is very much a postmodern culture. This is also true for the United States, although it has a larger and stronger Christian subculture. Throughout Europe, church attendance has declined drastically in the last two decades. In England of the 1850s, 39 percent of the population could be found in church on Sundays. By 1979 this had fallen to less than 12 percent, and by 1998 it was down to 7.5, a total of less than four million out of a population of fifty million. The latest trends suggest that not only is the decline continuing, but it is increasing.

The Salvation Army has not been immune to this deterioration. Since the mid–twentieth century, the number of soldiers in the United Kingdom has fallen from 120,000 to somewhere around 38,000. In addition, the demographic profile of the Army in the UK is such that we are one of the "grayest" denominations in the nation. Nevertheless, I'm delighted to say that the picture is not entirely bleak. There are "hot spots" where good things are happening and a radical new approach to youth ministry has been initiated and should make a considerable difference. But overall, there is no denying that the problem is serious.

The situation appears to be better in the United States, where church attendance is considerably higher. While Black, Hispanic, and Asian congregations have been growing largely because of immigration, there is also significant decline, especially in major denominations. In 1968, eleven mainline denominations accounted for 13 percent of the entire population. By 1993, the same denominations could only claim less than 8 percent. If this trend continues, they will not exist by the year 2032.

The tremendous trust that the American public places in The Salvation Army, and the resulting financial support, mean that the Army's future as

14

a social service agency is secure. But in general, the Army's congregations are small and have not grown in proportion to our social and community work, suggesting that the phenomenon of the declining church may also be a foreseeable reality for the Army in the United States.

The natural reaction of the churches in a time of seemingly chaotic change is to reaffirm their natural conservatism and hold doggedly to the status quo. What is needed is quite the opposite. It is indeed time for change. The challenge is to distinguish between those things that cannot change—the proclamation of the gospel of grace and our commitment to a lost world in humble service—and those that must.

The truth is that the death of the church in the West is no longer a matter for debate. The only question is, what kind of death is it to be? If our priority is to hold on to our denominational traditions, our outmoded structures, and the last vestiges of our prestige, it will be the kind of death that leads to our demise. In preserving the status quo, we will have denied the gospel. If, however, it is the kind of death that willingly gives up all for the sake of Jesus Christ and His gospel, it will lead to resurrection and as yet undreamed of opportunities. The seed must die to produce the plant that bears fruit, but seed and fruit look very different. The one thing that is certain about the church of the future is that it will look very different from that of the present.

Invitation to Incarnation

Referencing a popular movie at the time, Tony Campolo once told church leaders: "The trouble with you today is that you have a 'Field of Dreams' theology! You think that 'if you build it, they will come.' You think that if you build a new program or a new facility, people will come. But Jesus never said that. Jesus told us to go!" Campolo was absolutely right. For far too long we have been asking the question, "How do we get people to come to church?" It is the wrong question. What we should be asking is, "How do we take the church and, more important, the Lord of the church to the people?"

We often feel on solid biblical ground when we reflect that so much of the gospel is couched in terms of invitation. But we have forgotten that invitation comes only after incarnation. The Lord who invites us to come to Him is the Lord who first of all came to us, who became one of us. That same Lord tells us that as the Father had sent Him, so He sends us to draw others to Him. More than ever we need to be an incarnational people.

We earn the right to invite people to join us only when we first identify with them, sharing their neighborhood and their needs. One of the most gratifying new churches for which I have pastoral responsibility is in a deprived area of Manchester, England. The once strong, traditional Salvation Army corps there died some years ago as the congregation moved to better parts of the city. But now an equally thriving church exists, led by four full-time workers and a dozen volunteers. Not only do they all worship and witness in that area but they also live there, involving themselves fully in the life of the community. The church looks nothing like the former corps, but it is far more effective because it is genuinely incarnational.

Maintenance to Mission

In Britain, back in the 1950s, owning a motor car was just coming within the reach of most ordinary people. It was quite common then to see the fortunate few car owners drive their car out of the garage, wipe it down with a chamois cloth, admire it for a few minutes, and then move it straight back into the garage! They were delighted to own a vehicle but seemed more concerned about maintenance than motoring. I have often thought that we look on the church as those immobile motorists looked on their cars—we are more concerned with maintenance than mission.

Years ago I shared a painful conversation with a faithful, hardworking Christian man. In discussing the direction that the church should take, he used a phrase I cannot forget. "My aim," he said, "is to *preserve an expression*. I want my kids to be able to take part in the same activities I participated in." I respected both his hard work and his honesty, but his is a philosophy that is tragically inadequate for a postmodern world. Even if it were possible to preserve the old ways—and I'm sure it isn't—the very success of such an approach would render us powerless to reach out to today's changing world.

Many churches, in fact, have recognized the pressing need to move away from maintenance and have switched their emphasis to a kind of marketing approach. They have defined the "target group" they hope to reach, identified the needs of that group, assessed their resources with which they hope to meet those needs, and made their worship services "seeker-friendly." A great deal can be said for this approach. It reminds us that the church, as one Archbishop of Canterbury expressed it, is the only society on earth that exists primarily for the benefit of nonmembers. It challenges us to make the gospel accessible to unchurched people, and it has done so successfully in different parts of the western world. But increasingly, wise leaders are recognizing that it does not go far enough.

The age in which we live demands not only that we move from maintenance and learn from the world of marketing, but also that we place our emphasis firmly on mission. The heart of mission lies in accepting the fact that God sends us into the world to proclaim His message of reconciliation and restoration for the entire creation through Jesus Christ. Of course, we need to speak prophetically to the world, declaring God's desire for righteousness and justice. But that prophetic stand should never lead us into a separation based on self-righteousness or into the isolation of our own religious subculture. We must be where people are, sharing their lives and entering fully into their world.

The move toward mission is risky; the danger is that the culture we seek to challenge and transform may actually squeeze us into its own mold. It is a risk, however, we can take—and must—if we hold fast to the three-fold nature of the Great Commission (Matthew 28:18–20).

First, we must remember that we go on the *authority* of Jesus.

> All authority in heaven and on earth has been given to Me.
> Therefore go and make disciples of all nations.

If we are serious about the gospel and our obedience to the Lord, we have no alternative but to move out in mission. Second, we must be committed to the *strategy* of Jesus.

> Go and make disciples of all nations, baptizing them in the name of the Father and of the Son and of the Holy Spirit, and teaching them to obey everything I have commanded you.

Our presence in the world is no mere dalliance with the spirit of the age or the prevailing culture of the time. We are here for a purpose—to confront men and women with the claims of Christ and bring them to joyful submission to His will.

Third, we must maintain an *intimacy* with Jesus to ensure that He remains our first love and greatest passion.

> And surely I will be with you always, to the very end of the age.

Only this relationship to our Lord will enable us to love the world as He does without being seduced and compromised by its values and mores.

Mission in a post–Christian, postmodern world can only be implemented effectively by a church prepared to follow her Lord by living dangerously, by giving up all pretense of status and prestige, by standing with the poor and marginalized, and by walking and talking with sinners of every condition. Like her Lord, she will be misunderstood and persecuted, not least by those who are most seemingly religious. Like her Lord, she may well face death and defeat but, like her Lord, she will surely discover that the road to Easter and Pentecost is revealed only to those who travel to Calvary.

Membership to Discipleship

When it comes to joining a church, the old paradigm was simple and logical enough in a world of slow change, where institutions were respected and people accepted the idea of an objective truth to which they had to subscribe. The first step was that you had to *believe*. That belief usually was more than a statement of faith in Jesus Christ as Lord and God; it meant an intellectual assent to a series of doctrinal statements set out by that particular denomination. The second step involved *behavior*. Again, this normally implied more than a simple re–orientation of one's lifestyle. It may have involved specific promises, such as abstinence from alcohol and tobacco. Often it meant adopting the unspoken but very definite sub-culture of the group, learning the appropriate religious jargon and wearing the right clothes. Only when you had affirmed belief and accepted the behavior could you move on to *belonging* to the church, to becoming a member with all the accompanying privileges.

The old paradigm worked well in the modern world. After all, it was the rational approach. It was tidy and suited the tenor of the times. The problem is that it won't work any longer in today's world, marked by its eclectic spirituality, consumer mentality, and deep suspicion of institutions. But that is not a cause for despair, for the challenge we face may lead us to a more biblical approach. Think of the original disciples being called by Jesus. They had no ready-made doctrinal statement, no fixed belief. They did not know that the One who called them was the divine Son of God who would die for them, rise again, pour out His Holy Spirit, and establish His Church. They just knew that there was something different about Jesus, and they were willing to risk everything to follow Him. Nor were they models of Christian behavior. In fact, a more unworthy group is hard to imagine—Judas the traitor, Thomas the doubter, Peter with the big mouth and the quick temper, James and John with their ruthless desire to have the most prominent place in the group. Despite all that, they followed—they belonged! The belief and the behavior arose—albeit slowly and imperfectly—out of the belonging.

That, I suggest, is the pattern for the church in a postmodern world. We must allow people to belong, and in so doing, they will begin to believe and behave. Of course, that's a messy and a dangerous approach. People will let us down. But it is the way that Jesus took. Effective churches in the twenty-first century will be solid at the core, knowing what they believe, sure of the standards and lifestyle toward which the gospel calls us; but they will also be more fluid at the edges, allowing people to come in and explore the gospel without having to negotiate a series of intellectual and cultural hurdles. John Drane, a professor of practical theology at the University of Aberdeen, Scotland, and adjunct professor in the School of Theology at Fuller Seminary in Pasadena, expresses it perfectly in his book *Cultural Change and Biblical Faith* (Paternoster Press).

> This will be a huge challenge to the status quo, for it will require us to put into reverse gear the way most of our churches operate. We typically invite people to believe first... and then, we say, you can belong to the community of God's people. The need of our culture, however, is for us to create a community where people can feel comfortable to belong, and then to be continuously challenging and encouraging one another in the belonging.

Bureaucrat to Apostle

When I was a young adult, The Salvation Army in Britain was a monolithic culture. Apart from different accents, an Army corps in the south of England would be fairly similar to one in Scotland. Apart from contrasts in members' economic status, an inner city corps was not that different from one in the more affluent suburbs. The style of worship, the denominational jargon, the navy blue uniform, even the architecture of the building, would leave you with no doubt as to where you were. That shared culture was preserved and fostered by the strongly hierarchical system under which the movement was governed. Instructions came down the line on all kinds of matters.

Over the years that control has lessened, and the shared culture has been diluted. Some corps remain very traditional, some are much more contemporary. Some reflect a charismatic style of worship, in some there is scarcely a uniform to be seen. There are many who lament the changes and, no doubt, there have been some losses. But the tide cannot—indeed, should not—be reversed. A "one–size–fits–all" approach will not work in a world that is culturally complex, ethnically varied, and influenced by consumer values. Nor will a strictly "top–down," bureaucratic style of government work in a world of unpredictable, discontinuous, and rapid change. It is no coincidence that denominations with a hierarchical, strongly centralized structure have suffered most in postmodern society.

Some would even suggest that denominations no longer have a place, that only local churches choosing to interconect for mission and outreach can meet the needs of our time. This assessment certainly holds some truth. Local congregations, motivated for mission, will have more in common with like–minded churches of other denominations who share their passion for the lost than with those in their own milieu content with the status quo. Denominations will still have a powerful role—perhaps even an increasing role—in the ongoing work of the church if they are willing to "flatten out" their structures and allow mission to drive their decisions.

The previously mentioned church that the Army planted in inner–city Manchester was set up in partnership with a Christian youth agency. Of the six or seven churches that partnered with the youth agency, none has done better than The Salvation Army in acquiring sufficient funding to enable the project to function with maximum effectiveness. That is because we are able to use our denominational structure to direct financial and personnel resources to the project. The project was not "controlled" in the traditional sense but was allowed to evolve into a style of worship and ministry that arose from the needs and nature of the community rather than from the traditional pattern of the Army.

This example has taught me an enormous lesson regarding the way denominations and denominational leaders must work. Some might say that we have lost control and, in one sense, they would be correct. But rather than control, we evaluate the effectiveness of the program, hold the team accountable for their ministry, and celebrate the uniqueness of the model. Whatever authority I have over the project derives not primarily from my position, but from the quality of my relationships with the team and the quantity of the resources we devote to the ministry.

Policy to Pragmatism

When I lived in southern California for almost five years, I learned a thing or two about earthquakes! I discovered that the authorities have ceased to rely on the science of earthquake prediction; it is simply too inexact a science with too many variables. Instead, they focus on earthquake pre-paredness. No one knows when the "big one" will come, but everyone needs to be ready if and when it does. Bridges and overpasses are being reinforced, citizens are encouraged to equip themselves with necessary supplies, and emergency services are prepared to respond at any time.

Although vision and strategy are essential, and will be discussed later in this book, enterprise and flexibility are as important as planning in this rapidly changing world. The effective church of the twenty-first century will be ready to abandon its carefully made plans, if need be, to respond to a new and unpredicted set of circumstances. Our policies must never be set in stone, and our programs and practices must ever remain fluid.

Pastor to Pioneer

A different kind of church inevitably demands a different kind of leader. Indeed, a shift in our understanding of leadership is required if we are to train, equip, and employ the men and women who will lead the church into the future. The old paradigm judged a leader's worth by his ability to function in several key areas:

> *He was expected to pastor the flock.* It was not uncommon for denominations to prescribe exactly how many hours the pastor should spend visiting the congregation in their homes. (Someone once observed cynically that too many congregations expect the pastor to be more of a sheepdog than a shepherd.)

> *He was expected to preach the word.* Many congregations still ask would-be pastors to deliver a sermon so that they can make a judgment on his ability to lead their church.

> *He was expected to play the part of the resident "holy man,"* representing the church in civic ceremonies and just being there at times of shared grief or rejoicing.

> *He was expected to preserve denominational traditions,* demonstrating his grasp of and allegiance to the theological emphases and the cultural mores of the church he served.

> *He was expected to preside over the "rites of passage,"* conducting marriages, christenings, dedications, and funerals— in colloquial terms, to hatch, match, and dispatch!

These roles properly and legitimately remain part of a leader's mandate. Preaching the Word and caring for the people will always be of enormous importance. But a new set of skills have been added without which a leader cannot be truly effective in the church today.

> *Today's leaders are managers of change.* Fewer and fewer churches will remain stable. Congregations will either grow or decline, and change will be a constant factor. Those with a penchant for preserving the status quo will not sit comfortably with the future style of leadership in the church.

> *Today's leaders are missiologists.* The study and practice of mission—how to reach out to a world whose values and viewpoints are very different from those of the Bible—is a vital skill. To remain pastors of the faithful is not enough; to become pioneers, boldly leading the people where the church has never gone before, is essential.

> *Today's leaders are masters of strategy.* Effective leaders have learned the skill of vision-casting, and we align everything with that vision to give the church clear focus and definite direction.

> *Today's leaders are merchants of spiritual commerce.* Strong leaders have learned to do business with today's age. We understand its culture, and we package the gospel as a diamond merchant displays his wares—not disguising them but placing them in settings where their beauty can best be appreciated. We are constantly asking ourselves, "What aspect of the gospel needs to shine out at this time to catch the eye and draw in those hungry for true worth and beauty?"

The church will be best served by leaders who are risk-takers, leaders who love the Lord of the church more than the institution of the church, leaders who are willing to sacrifice the Body of Christ today just as Jesus sacrificed Himself two thousand years ago for the sake of the lost, leaders who are willing to discover life through death. As we know in our hearts, that has always been the only way for the church to be true to her calling.

three

The Christlike Leader

**To become Christlike is the only thing in the world worth caring for,
the thing before which every ambition of man is folly
and all lower achievement vain.**

Henry Drummond

Peter Block is a best-selling author of several books on management and leadership. In *Stewardship* (Berrett–Koehler Publishers), he makes an astute observation:

> There is something in the way leaders define themselves that inevitably becomes self–congratulatory and over–controlling. We expect leaders to choose service over self–interest, but it seems the choice is rarely made. Successful leaders begin to believe that a key task is to re–create themselves down through the organization.

Block's comment highlights the great dangers that often accompany leadership—the dangers of becoming self–important, seeking to control others, and failing to recognize the worth of individuals.

If those traits are undesirable in leaders of industry or government, they are even more dangerous in those who aspire to leadership in the Christian Church. Indeed, they are a denial of the gospel of grace and love we are called to share with a needy world. It might be argued by some that if a man or woman is competent in the skills of leadership, then character and personal integrity matter little; but that is an argument that just doesn't cut it with Christian leaders whose model for leadership is Jesus Christ Himself. What kind of leader was Jesus? Accordingly, what kind of leaders should we be?

Open to the Leadings of God

The life and leadership of Jesus were characterized by what can best be described as a quality of openness. His life was a channel through which the love and power of His Father flowed freely to everyone with whom He made contact. Christian leaders need to discover the secret of that openness, without which spiritual leadership can never become a reality.

LISTEN TO THE WORD OF GOD

At the beginning of His earthly ministry in the loneliness of the desert, Jesus underwent a time of intense temptation, to which leaders are particularly susceptible. He was tempted to use His power for personal gain by turning stones into bread. Satan suggested that Jesus test the providential care of God and sway the crowd with a spectacular display of the supernatural by leaping from the pinnacle of the Temple and have angels catch Him. Jesus was also told that He would enjoy world domination if He would offer worship to the evil one. But He stood firm, resisting the devil's seductions by planting His feet on the sure foundation of the Word of God (Matthew 4:1–11).

It was not just that Jesus knew and could quote Scripture but that Scripture governed the way He thought and lived. For example, His subsequent ministry embodied the Servant Songs in the prophesy of Isaiah, contradicting the expectations of his contemporaries. While they looked for a Messiah to rule by military might and cast out the hated Roman oppressors, Jesus listened to the Word of God and imbibed its truths and precepts, thus fulfilling the prophet's description of the Messiah.

Christlike leaders who are open to the leadings of God give much time to the study of God's Word. When a scholar once set out to translate the New Testament, someone asked his son, "I wonder what your father will make of the Gospels." The young man astutely responded, "I wonder what the Gospels will make of my father." There is a place for studying the Word of God, there is a place for preparing sermons from the Word of God, but Christian leaders give the greatest place to reflecting on what God has to say through His Word in order that their character and values may be shaped by that Word.

LEARN TO WAIT ON GOD

We live in a busy world. And the man or woman who accepts the call to leadership will be among the busiest. Too often such activity becomes frenetic and leads to bitterness and breakdown. When we read the gospels two things almost leap off the page: The first is that Jesus faced constant demands on His time. Crowds called for His attention wherever He went. The second is that He was never hurried, never ran on the treadmill of activity. He had learned to wait on His Father. Effective spiritual leaders need to model themselves after Jesus in this respect. In the book *The Heart of a Great Pastor* (Regal Books), H. B. London Jr. and Neil B. Wiseman beautifully and clearly express the kind of life we need to cultivate. They call it "a God–permeated life" and describe it like this:

> [It] means getting together often with God. To use teenage language, we hang out with Him. This God–closeness, like falling in love, creates attentiveness, togetherness and warmth. This deepening intimacy with God opens our eyes to see amazing mysteries of grace and provides fulfilment throughout a lifetime of ministry. . . . It is like an electrical conduit through which divine enablement flows through us. [We] experience such empowerment as [we] welcome the One T. S. Eliot described in his prayer: "Oh, my soul, be prepared for the coming of the Stranger, Be prepared for Him who knows how to ask questions."

Leadership on the Axis of Change

LOOK AT THE WORLD AROUND YOU

The openness of Jesus did not lead Him to a spirituality that left the world behind. His conversation and communication were filled with illustrations and insights drawn from the world around Him. He knew that its beauties and wonders reflected the beauties and wonders of heaven itself. Like Gerard Manley Hopkins, the great Jesuit poet, He believed that "the world is charged with the grandeur of God." He constantly drew eternal truth from the created universe with its changing seasons and meaningful mysteries of death and renewal. Eugene H. Peterson encourages us in *The Contemplative Pastor* (Word Publishing) to "read the book of creation with . . . care and intensity," reminding us:

> Without a firm rooting in creation, religion is always drifting off into some kind of pious sentimentalism or sophisticated intellectualism. . . . The physical is holy. It is extremely significant that in the opening sentences of the Bible, God speaks a world of energy and matter into being. . . . Apart from creation, covenant has no structure, no context, no rootage in reality.

In sum, the leader who is open to God will discern His leadings through His written Word, in the intimacy of communion with Him, and in the glory of His creation.

Filled with the Spirit of God

We can gain many insights into the nature of leadership from the worlds of business and politics. We find skills to be learned and techniques to be mastered, which will help us become more effective leaders. But there is one distinction of spiritual leadership that cannot be drawn from reading or derived from any case study. Jesus embodied the supreme leader because He was perfectly filled with the Spirit of God. His will was to do His Father's will, His words were His Father's words, His way of life and love was the way His Father desired.

We fall far short of His perfection, yet we are nevertheless called to lead as He led—to draw men to our Father God, to deliver His words, to do His will, and to walk His way. We, too, must be filled with the Spirit of God, and to that openness must be added an obedience to what God reveals and an eagerness—an insatiable hunger—for all that God is. In the book *The Eternal Promise* (Hodder & Stoughton), Thomas R. Kelly brings this issue into sharp focus with pertinent and probing questions:

> Ask yourself: "Am I down in the flaming center of God? Have I come into the deeps where the soul meets with God and knows His love and power? Have I discovered God as a living Immediacy, a sweet Presence, and a stirring, life-renovating Power within me?"

After openness and obedience, there is only one condition that we must meet if we want to be filled with the Spirit of God—we must want it and ask for it. Jesus Himself promised that if we, with all our faults, know how to give good gifts to our children, how much more will our heavenly Father give the Holy Spirit to those who ask Him? (Luke 11:13). The supreme purpose of a leader is to lead, and the supreme purpose of the Christian leader is to lead others to Christ. Only Spirit-filled men and women can exercise that kind of leadership.

Committed to the Purposes of God

I walk faster than anyone else in our family, so I am usually ahead if we are walking together. Unfortunately, I also have a bad sense of direction, and the two traits don't fit well together. One of our daughters often says, "Dad always takes the lead, even though he's got no idea where he's going!" Alas, the same could be said of some would-be leaders, and the results can be disastrous. Leaders need to know the direction in which they are taking their people. That was certainly true of Jesus' leadership.

THE ABILITY TO FOCUS

Jesus was committed to obeying the will of His heavenly Father, and He devoted Himself to discerning and doing God's will. As a result, His life had focus and a sense of direction from which nothing could distract Him. Mark's Gospel tells us how, again and again, Jesus warned His disciples of

His impending death and the cost of sacrifice. His strongest rebuke was delivered to Peter when he tried to dissuade Jesus from that path (Mark 8:31–33), and nowhere in the gospels do we see His awesome authority more clearly than in His final journey to Jerusalem and certain death:

> They were on their way up to Jerusalem, with Jesus leading the way, and the disciples were astonished, while those who followed were afraid. (Mark 10:32)

The world still looks for that kind of authority in its leaders, for men and women who know where they are going and who are willing to pay the price. During the early days of World War II, Winston Churchill addressed a worried Parliament and a beleaguered Britain with the words "I have nothing to offer but blood, toil, tears and sweat." Whatever its views of his political stance on other matters, on May 13, 1940, the nation recognized that here was a man with the focus and firmness to see them through the dark days of conflict. The authentic voice of leadership had been heard, and people felt instinctively that they could travel the dangerous road ahead with such a leader. The Christian leader who is committed to the purpose of God and who will pay the price of the cross will ultimately inspire confidence in others who fear the future and long to travel in the company of a trusted guide.

THE INVITATION TO FOLLOW

One of many remarkable things about the leadership of Jesus is that people were willing to leave everything and follow Him. However some may try to explain those verses in the first chapter of Mark's Gospel— Jesus may have had some previous contact with Simon and the other fishermen; they may have heard about Him from others—it remains a cause for amazement that, in the face of economic uncertainty and an unknown future, they left, without a moment's hesitation, the relative security of a family business and a network of friends to follow a penniless Rabbi.

The only explanation is that there was something different about this man. These aspects of a spiritual leader—His openness and obedience to the Father, His infilling of the Spirit of God, His commitment to the will and purpose of God—gave Him an authority and an attractive quality that drew others to Him. When He said, "Come, follow Me," He was simply articulating the invitation that He had already given by His life.

In one sense, Christian leaders constantly point not to themselves but to Christ. In another sense, they inevitably call others to follow them. The challenge is to live such Christlike lives that when people follow us, they are led to follow Christ. Paul expressed this truth in his letter to the Thessalonians: "You know how we lived among you for your sake. You became imitators of us and of the Lord" (1:5,6). The mark of the effective Christian leader is that his life is an invitation to follow. The closer others come to him, the closer they come to Christ.

THE CAPACITY TO FORGIVE

Unsuccessful leaders often complain about the people they are forced to work with. If only they had a better team, they lament, they could do so much more. When we read the gospels we find that Jesus had a very different approach to leadership. Despite the fact that He spent an entire night in prayer before calling on the twelve men to form the inner circle of His followers, Jesus still chose an unlikely group. They included Simon Peter, who usually spoke before he thought; Matthew the tax collector, who had collaborated with the occupying Roman government; James and John, who were so fiery tempered that they were nicknamed "the Sons of Thunder"; Thomas, afflicted with a pessimism that made it difficult for him to exercise faith; and Judas Iscariot, whose name has become a byword for treacherous disloyalty.

Those were the men on whose faith and commitment the Christian Church would be built; those were the men who would turn the world upside-down. And it was because Jesus was the greatest example of the kind of leader who looks not for perfection but for potential, who does not simply discard a man or woman because of past sins and mistakes but patiently recognizes that people represent a long-term, slowly maturing investment. In short, Jesus had an infinite capacity to forgive. When His disciples challenged Him to be specific, He refused to put any limit on forgiveness. Don't forgive seven times, He told them. Make it seventy times seven (Matthew 18:22). Don't keep count, and never give up on people.

That kind of leadership liberates people to become, by God's grace, what they could never otherwise be. Simon Peter is an obvious example of the power of forgiving leadership. Without forgiveness this man, who denied Jesus at His hour of greatest need, would have been discarded; without forgiveness this man, who fled in the face of danger, would have been judged unworthy as a follower. But the risen Lord sought him out, asked for his love, and called him to be a true shepherd of the flock (John 21:15–19). Instead of being rejected, he became a rock on whose faith and subsequent leadership the Christian Church was built.

Christlike leaders, committed to the purposes of God, have no illusions about the frailty of the people whom they serve. Neither are they in any doubt about the power of forgiveness to restore those who would otherwise be lost and to make leaders of those who would otherwise be dismissed as failures. It is the capacity to forgive, as much as anything else, that will authenticate the Christlike leader. As Alice Cary expressed it: "Nothing in this lost world bears the impress of the Son of God so surely as forgiveness."

four

The Servant Leader

I don't know what your destiny will be, but one thing I know: The ones among you who will be really happy are those who have sought and found how to serve.

Albert Schweitzer

There is a saying in my native Scotland which runs: "It's better felt than telt." Loosely translated it means that often the most profound truths are more easily recognized and experienced than analyzed and explained. That is certainly the case with servant leadership. We know it the moment we see it in action, and we can detect its opposite even more quickly; but the task of describing what it means to be a servant leader often defeats us. Of course, we can always say that actions speak louder than words and leave it at that, but, since none of us—apart from Jesus Himself—is perfectly possessed of a servant heart, we might easily miss a vital part of the picture. The task is not impossible, however, for the principles of servant leadership are found in the pages of Scripture.

Surrender to Christ

> But whatever was to my profit I now consider loss for the sake of Christ. What is more, I consider everything a loss compared to the surpassing greatness of knowing Christ Jesus my Lord, for whose sake I have lost all things. (Philippians 3:7,8)

We may choose to live for many things. We may be sold out to personal wealth or fame, but that will ultimately cause us to become selfish. We may be sold out to a good cause, but that will ultimately render us hard and uncaring toward others if we neglect integrity in the means we use and forget the value of those with whom we work. We may even be sold out to religion and the church, but that will ultimately make us proud and self-righteous. It is only when we are sold out to Jesus Christ, when our hearts are passionate for Him and for the world for which He died, that we will truly have the attitude of a servant, the attitude of Jesus Himself.

Few people have exemplified that kind of service more than Mother Theresa of Calcutta. When she died, millions mourned the passing of this woman whose quality of leadership shone just as brightly in the most distinguished company as it did in the mean city streets where she served with her order of nuns. It is not difficult to discover the secret of her success: She was utterly and passionately committed to Jesus Christ. Quoted from *The London Times*, she gives eloquent expression to servant leadership in this simple testimony:

> By blood and origin I am an Albanian.
> My citizenship is Indian.
> I am a Catholic nun.
> As to my calling, I belong to the world.
> As to my heart, I belong entirely to the heart of Jesus.

That is the point at which all true servant leadership begins. Whatever the precise nature of our ministry might be, our first and greatest allegiance must be to Jesus Christ.

Self–sacrifice for the Church

> Now I rejoice in what was suffered for you, and I fill up in
> my flesh what is still lacking in regard to Christ's afflictions,
> for the sake of His body, which is the church. I have become
> its servant, by the commission God gave me. (Colossians
> 1:24,25)

I can still remember the sense of shock I felt when I read these verses
carefully for the first time. What was Paul thinking when he wrote, "I fill
up in my flesh what is still lacking in regard to Christ's afflictions"? Surely
his theology was better than that! Didn't he know that Jesus died once for
all, that His atoning work on the cross is complete, that nothing needs to
be added? But then I recalled a conversation I shared with a colleague, a
minister in another denomination, whose congregation had been causing
him a great deal of heartache. He told me how he had struggled until one
day it dawned on him that this was his calling—to be Christ to his people,
that the cross had to be a reality if he was to be a servant leader, that
self–sacrifice for the sake of the church was part of the deal. As I reflected
on that conversation, Paul's words began to make sense.

That certainly doesn't mean that a servant leader is afraid of confrontation or that he puts up with anything for the sake of a quiet life. But
it does mean that—because of his love for the Lord of the church, because
of his conviction that the church is central to God's great plan to bring salvation to a lost world, because of his vision of what the church is called to
be at her best—he willingly gives himself to the church in costly service.
Much of the secret of Bill Hybels' effective leadership surely lies in his high
view of the local church, as he states in his book *Courageous Leadership*
(Zondervan Publishing House):

> There is nothing like the local church when it is working
> right. Its beauty is indescribable. Its power is breathtaking. Its
> potential is unlimited. It comforts the grieving and heals the
> broken in the context of community. It builds bridges to
> seekers and offers truth to the confused. It provides

resources for those in need and opens its arms to the forgotten, the downtrodden, the disillusioned. It breaks the chains of addictions, frees the oppressed, and offers belonging to the marginalized of this world. Whatever the capacity for human suffering, the church has a greater capacity for healing and wholeness.

Any man or woman with leadership in their DNA would give their life in willing self-sacrifice for a church like that!

Service to All

There is a ruthless honesty about the gospels. Nowhere is that more true than in the salutary tale of the sons of Zebedee. James and his brother John were ambitious, no doubt about that. In fact, their ambition led them to offer the worst prayer ever made to Jesus. "Teacher," they said, "we want You to do for us whatever we ask." There was nothing about seeking the will of God—just an undisguised attempt to use prayer to their own ends. But it gets worse! They wanted the best places in the kingdom of God, each brother sitting on a regal throne on either side of Jesus. No wonder the other disciples began to feel indignant.

But Jesus countered with a question. Could they share His baptism and drink His cup—were they willing to follow His example and share His fate? They glibly answered that they could. At that point Jesus spelled out for them the greatest principle of leadership ever expressed:

> Jesus called them together and said, "You know that those who are regarded as rulers of the Gentiles lord it over them, and their high officials exercise authority over them. Not so with you. Instead, whoever wants to become great among you must be your servant, and whoever wants to be first must be slave of all. For even the Son of Man did not come to be served, but to serve, and to give His life as a ransom for many." (Mark 10:42–45)

This is where the rubber meets the road. Leaders who follow Jesus must be servant leaders, and servant leaders must be willing to serve! That might seem to be stating the obvious, but it's amazing how hard it is for us to grasp. There is no place among the followers of Jesus for leaders with a "top table" mentality. I cannot remember who penned these words, but the following paragraph challenges me every time I read it:

> Great leaders have a passion for equality. History defines examples such as Alexander the Great sharing his food with his men, calling them by their first names, marching along with them in the heat, and being the first over the wall in battle. . . . Contrast this with a management style which finds equality repugnant, where promotion, perks, privilege and power are the name of the game, and awe and reverence for rank are everything.

The One whom we follow settled the issue for us once and for all when He took the towel and basin and performed the task of a humble slave in washing the dusty feet of His disciples. The command that followed His action must form the creed of every Christian leader; it must be the rock on which we stand when position, popularity, or prestige would entice us:

> "Do you understand what I have done for you?" He asked them. "You call me 'Teacher' and 'Lord,' and rightly so for that is what I am. Now that I, your Lord and Teacher, have washed your feet, you also should wash one another's feet. I have set you an example that you should do as I have done for you. (John 13:12–14)

Submission to Others

Submission is a tricky word. It first entered my vocabulary years ago when, as a twelve–year–old boy, I used to watch wrestling on television. The commentator would repeat the formula like a mantra before each bout: "Two falls, two submissions, or a knockout to decide the winner." A submission was the point at which one of the contestants would "give in" to his stronger opponent. Consequently, I grew up with the idea that submission was for softies—definitely not for leaders!

But the biblical meaning of the word is quite different: "Submit to one another out of reverence for Christ" (Ephesians 5:21). Paul's words to the Ephesians do not constitute a command to let bullies have their way. Rather, as Eugene H. Peterson renders it in *The Message*, this is a call for us to "be courteously reverent to one another" out of respect for Christ. What that means, in effect, is that in every relationship—and especially those in which we have authority over another person—we should treat that person with the respect and honor we would give to Jesus Christ Himself if He were standing before us.

Servant leaders demonstrate submissiveness by their courtesy, their availability, and their accountability. Their leadership is characterized by conversation more than by coercion, by discussion more than demand, and by consensus more than command. They seek to direct the credit to their team rather than claim it for themselves. They are recognizable by the way in which they are concerned for the welfare of their people at least as much as for the successful completion of their projects. They have listening ears, attentive eyes, and caring hearts.

Suffering for a Purpose

> The life of a soul-saver is the grandest, merriest, strangest life that can be lived on earth—the life of Jesus lived over again in us. It will cost you all, but it will be a good bargain at that!

So wrote George Scott Railton, The Salvation Army's first commissioner. His biographer, Bernard Watson, describes Railton's words in the book *Soldier Saint* (The Salvation Army) as "Franciscan," linking sacrifice with merriment. Without a doubt, Railton shared with Saint Francis a profound understanding that those who follow Christ must often reach joy through suffering. Those who seek to lead like Jesus will certainly need to face suffering, but such suffering is purposeful and character building. Again we turn to Scripture to discover how such suffering is instructive.

38

Facing failure

Elijah was a great servant of God and a powerful leader of Israel. But, like many a leader since, he knew times of defeat. His dramatic encounter with the prophets of Baal had left him exhausted and, when he received a message from Jezebel threatening his life, he fell into a deep depression. It was his lowest point as a man and as a leader of God's people. He had just stood alone against 400 prophets of Baal and had seen God move powerfully and miraculously. Now all that meant nothing to him as he fled for his life, afraid of the threats of one woman.

Elijah had gone from dramatic success to abysmal failure in just a few days. But it is in this place of failure that he encounters God in a new way as he hears His "still, small voice." It is here that he sees his self-pitying attitude and acknowledges that he is not the only faithful follower of the true God. It is here that he learns more of God's strategy and the part that he must play (1 Kings 19:9–18).

Albert Orsborn, who became the sixth general of The Salvation Army, was appointed a divisional commander while still a comparatively young man. A year later, when he heard that his division was to be subdivided, he fell into a mood of depression and rebellion. He carried on with his work but lost all sense of the presence and power of God. To compound matters, he fell while running to catch a bus in a busy London street and damaged his knee. He was in a place of failure, just as real as that of Elijah. But, while recovering in a convalescent home, he heard a snippet of an old gospel song from an adjoining room:

Nothing from His altar I would keep . . .

He yielded to the presence and persuasion of the Holy Spirit and began to write one of his own most poignant hymns, "Saviour, If My Feet Have Faltered," which begins:

Saviour, if my feet have faltered
On the pathway of the cross,
If my purposes have altered
Or my gold be turned to [mixed with] dross.

O forbid me not Thy service,
Keep me yet in Thy employ,
Pass me through a sterner cleansing
If I may but give Thee joy!

All my work is for the Master,
He is all my heart's desire;
O that He may count me faithful
In the day that tries by fire.

FACING ATTACK

On the night Jesus shared His final meal with His disciples before trial and crucifixion, He spoke to Simon Peter words that contained a prophecy, a promise, and a challenge:

Simon, Simon, Satan has asked to sift you as wheat. But I have prayed for you, Simon, that your faith may not fail. And when you have turned back, strengthen your brothers. (Luke 22:31,32)

Peter needed to know, as does every leader, that he would be under attack. It's inevitable, part of the deal, the strategy of the evil one. For Peter, that attack came in the temptation to deny Jesus in the face of questions of a servant girl. But attack can come in many forms—sexual sin, bitterness against a colleague, despair when things go wrong, compromised principles, and a thousand other temptations. And yet with the prophecy comes the promise that Jesus is praying for us. We have spiritual resources. Unlike Peter, we do not need to succumb. And from those attacks—those that overwhelm us and those we resist—come opportunities and challenges to strengthen our brothers and sisters.

Oddly enough, confession of failure is often as powerful in strengthening others as testimony to victory. When Gordon MacDonald wrote *Ordering Your Private World*, his wise counsel strengthened thousands of Christian leaders around the globe. A few years later MacDonald wrote that, despite his accumulated wisdom and counsel to others, he had fallen into sin and had failed to live up to biblical standards.

Ironically, MacDonald's confession and account of his subsequent journey of repentance and restoration did at least as much good as his earlier writings. Servant leaders have resources to draw from when attacked, and when we fail—as we all do at some point—even that failure can be used to strengthen others.

FACING CRITICISM

Leadership and uninterrupted popularity just don't fit together. Servant leadership is not soft leadership. In February 2003, a television news program in Britain carried a report of a speech by Prime Minister Tony Blair, in which he highlighted one of the challenges of leadership: "In the end, I've got to make a decision, and that's the difference between leadership and commentary." Leaders who refuse to make decisions are leaders in name only. Leaders who make decisions—particularly the hard or unpopular ones—will face criticism. They will be misunderstood, misquoted, and misjudged. But although it's a lonely place to be, the truth will come through.

The Apostle Paul was often attacked for his tough, uncompromising leadership in the early church and for his determination that no ceremony or ritual should ever become a barrier to non–Jews coming to faith in Christ. He faced ferocious criticism; even Peter was once numbered among his opponents (Galatians 2:11–21). The outcome of the debate (and consequential judgment of history on Paul) must have seemed bleak at the time. But centuries later the survival and success of the Christian Church throughout the world is a living demonstration of the truth for which Paul fought so hard. The man who described himself as "the least of the apostles" would not yield on the truth of the gospel. He stands as an example for all time of servant leadership that pays the price of unpopularity.

Paul's further description of himself in the introduction to his letter to the Christian Church in Rome suitably concludes this chapter. If it describes what Paul was, it also defines what we must become. If it is an expression of humility, it is also an exhortation to greatness. If ultimately became Paul's noblest epitaph, it must also become our highest ambition. In his own words, he was "a servant of Jesus Christ" (Romans 1:1).

five

The Consistent Leader

**If my private world is in order, it will be because I have chosen
to press Sabbath peace into the rush and routine of my daily life
in order to find the rest God prescribed for Himself and all of humanity.**

Gordon MacDonald, Ordering Your Private World

I met "John" at a civic event. I didn't recognize the man, but he obviously wanted to speak to me. After only a few minutes of conversation, I realized who he was. I had heard of him for almost as long as I have been in ministry, and I had heard the story of his "fall from grace" and his hasty departure from Christian leadership some years previously. As he spoke, the hurt and bitterness of those years of frustration poured out in a torrent of words. He admitted that he had done wrong but insisted that he had been misunderstood and that others had been at least as much at fault. He was still contemplating possible legal action to clear his name and to ensure that others took their share of the blame.

I sensed again the pain that I always feel when I am in the presence of a "leadership casualty." Leadership is a costly business, and many would–be leaders do not last the course. Sometimes they simply find the path too hard and choose to do something less demanding. Like "John," there are other instances where good men and women are overtaken by a moral or spiritual disaster that brings their ministry to a tragic, untimely end. Sadly, in so many cases the pitfalls could have been avoided with more care from the fallen leader and greater support from friends and colleagues. God needs leaders who will be there for the long haul and finish the race.

Leaders Can Burn Out

"Burn out" is one of the characteristic phrases of our age. It is also an apt description of how it feels to reach that point where the pace and demands of life render us incapable of functioning, where we simply give up because we no longer have the physical, emotional, or spiritual energy to carry on. Leaders probably suffer from burn out more than most, despite the fact that the greatest leader of all set a very different example. Author Richard A. Swenson points out in his book *The Overload Syndrome* (Navpress):

> We pay a price for the pace at which we live. The late French historian Jacques Ellul commented, "No one knows where we are going, the aim of life has been forgotten, the end has been left behind. Man has set out at a tremendous speed— to go nowhere." Have you ever noticed that Jesus never seemed to be in a hurry? Jesus understood that busyness, productivity, and efficiency are speed words, not Kingdom words. At times they are appropriate values, but they are never transcendent. Jesus understood that meditation, wisdom, and worship are slow, mellow, and deep.

Leaders Can Drop Out

In the previous chapter we acknowledged the fact that all leaders encounter failure and criticism, which can result in disappointment and disillusionment. If we don't know how to cope with such setbacks, they can lower our morale to such an extent that we become just another sorry statistic in the long list of those who have dropped out of ministry and leadership. If there is anything sadder than seeing a leader drop out, it is seeing a leader who stays at his post but has lost motivation and vision and simply goes through the motions of the task. The antidote to "drop-out syndrome" is to view a seemingly impossible situation from the perspective of Jesus Himself. In *The Heart of a Great Pastor*, London and Wiseman write:

> Jesus viewed potential from two perspectives: while using a towel to wash dirty feet, and from the cross. God usually assigns us to a place where we are most needed. . . . God may need us in a tough place where the salary is low and the housing is limited. Perhaps He will assign us to places of urban decay, social violence or moral desperation. . . . He might want us to serve brutal, greedy, exploitative people because we are their only hope. . . . Let's face it, pastors throughout the long, stirring march of Christian history have often bloomed best in moral barnyards. When a pastor begins to evaluate potential from Jesus' perspective, every congregation possesses extraordinary possibilities.

Leaders Can Fall Out

When I was young I imagined that there must be a special department in hell where Satan's cleverest demons are trained in techniques of sophisticated temptation to trap and ensnare Christian leaders. I was wrong! When Christian leaders fall into sin and out of leadership, they fall for the age-old temptations—power, sex, and money.

A leader can be drawn into sin in many ways; therefore, we need to be constantly on our guard. There are especially vulnerable times—when we are tired and depressed, when we allow bitterness to creep into our thinking, when we neglect the spiritual disciplines that preserve our intimacy with God, when we succumb to the seductions of flattery, when we are conscious of failure, or—even more dangerous—when we are seemingly at our most successful.

John C. Maxwell, in his book *The Twenty-One Indispensable Qualities of a Leader* (Thomas Nelson Publishers), counsels four courses of action that will help leaders avoid "fall out."

> *Search for cracks.* Spend time looking at the major areas of your life (work, marriage, family, service, etc.) and identify where you might have cut corners, compromised, or let people down. Write every instance you can recall from the past two months.
>
> *Look for patterns.* Examine the instances that you noted. Is there a particular area where you have a weakness, or do you have a type of problem that keeps surfacing? Detecting patterns will help you diagnose character weaknesses.
>
> *Face the music.* The beginning of character repair comes when you face your flaws, apologize, and deal with the consequences of your actions.
>
> *Rebuild.* Once you identify areas of weakness, create a plan that will prevent you from making the same mistakes again.

Leaders Can Sell Out

Most of us set out in our youth full of ideals, believing that we really could change the world. As the years passed, idealism was tempered by realism, and that is not a bad thing. Leaders need to live in the real world. They need to know that no victory this side of heaven is ever total. They need to be aware that no task is ever fully complete. And finally, they need to remember the words of Jesus—that the best of us are "unprofitable stewards." The problem arises when realism degenerates into cynicism, when passionate dreams are jettisoned and high principles are compromised.

Some time ago I attended a meeting with other church leaders, in which we discussed where we had been and what we had done on the previous Sunday. One of my colleagues—a highly respected figure with a national profile—said sadly, "On Sunday a man stood up and prayed for revival. It seemed strange to hear that prayer. Years ago I prayed for revival in our nation. Then I stopped doing that and prayed for the renewal of the church. Now I don't think I even pray for that anymore. It made me wonder how far I have compromised over the years." It was a telling moment, and I suspect that in the ensuing silence everyone present was searching their hearts and their consciences. Ultimately the only antidote to selling out to pressures around us is to be sold out to the calling and conviction within us.

Leaders Can Spread Out

We're all familiar with "middle-aged spread," a condition that afflicts those in their forties when the waistline expands and nothing fits as it used to. Of course, the condition is neither inevitable nor terminal and can be overcome by sensible eating and regular exercise. Middle-aged spread, however, is not simply a physical problem; it has its emotional and behavioral equivalents, as well. It can happen to leaders who still possess the same abilities but who lose focus, who are driven along by a multiplicity of tasks that bombard us in our extremely busy world. In fact, it threatens all of us who succumb to the unrealistic expectations of those who believe the myth of the omni-competent super-leader.

Too many of us have no time to lead because we are distracted by the thousand different tasks and responsibilities that others have placed on us or that we have gathered ourselves. When this happens, we need to remind ourselves of our truest passion and get back to the urgency of the need, the immediacy of our calling, and the intimacy of our relationship with the One who called us.

The good news is that all of the problems we have listed—burn out, drop out, fall out, sell out, and spread out—can be kept at bay with the right kind of discipline and dedication.

Leaders Live with MAPS

Common sense tells us that leaders need to learn how best to manage their time, but good time management by itself is not enough. Time management makes us conscious of our minutes and how to use them well; to state the same thing in a different way, time management is all about how we spend our time. What we need, however, is something that will help us spend our lives most effectively; and, in order to do that, we must learn to live not by the minutes but by a map. We need to find a direction for our lives that identifies the principles by which we live and the priorities we want to achieve. Four areas of focus need to be addressed—Mission, Aim, Priorities, and Scrutiny (MAPS).

Mission: Why am I here?

The first questions that leaders need to ask are the biggest ones anyone can ask: "Why am I here? What is the grand design behind my very being? What is my purpose in life?" A wise colleague asked me many years ago, "What is it you do, that when you do it, you know that's why God created you?" For Christian leaders, our primary mission is found in the will and work of God as revealed in the Bible. More specifically, it is offered in the two passages of Scripture we know as the Great Commandment and the Great Commission:

> "The most important [commandment]," answered Jesus, "is this: 'Hear, O Israel, the Lord our God, the Lord is one. Love the Lord your God with all your heart and with all your soul and with all your mind and with all your strength.' The second is this: 'Love your neighbor as yourself.' There is no commandment greater than these." (Luke 12:29–31)

> Then Jesus came to them and said, "All authority in heaven and on earth has been given to me. Therefore go and make disciples of all nations, baptizing them in the name of the Father and of the Son and of the Holy Spirit, and teaching them to obey everything I have commanded you. And surely I am with you always, to the end of the age. (Matthew 28:18–20)

These are the touchstones for all that we do. Everything else we do is an outcome of that mission. Our mission is the foundation of the map we follow; it is the compass to which we look for direction. It is the magnetic

North which steadies and guides us toward absolute devotion to God and our neighbor, which will find its fullest expression in sharing the good news of the gospel and presenting the challenge of discipleship to all people.

Aim: Where do I want to go?

It is only when I am clear about my mission that I can decide my aim. Where do I want to go? What are the tasks I need to do, and what are the goals I need to complete in order to fulfill my mission in life?

Like most people in leadership, I am invited to serve on a variety of committees. In truth, attending meetings can become a full-time job! So I am constantly asking myself, "If I attend this committee, will it further the mission to which I am committed?" I also find it useful to test what I am doing by regularly using the following criteria:

> *Urgent and important:* All of us need to spend time working in this area. There are tasks that are simply part of the job or issues that arise to which we need to react—crises to be resolved, problems to be solved, deadlines to be met.

> *Urgent but not important:* Leaders particularly need to control this area and, as far as possible, eliminate from their lives. I have heard it described as "the area of deception"— it is the needless interruptions, the unnecessary reports, the pointless meetings, and the minor issues. Leaders who have no map with which to work can spend most of their time here—doing a great deal but achieving very little.

> *Not urgent and not important:* To be avoided at all costs, this is the area of needless trivia—spending time on the web looking at sites that have nothing to do with the task at hand, lingering on the telephone when proper courtesy has been expressed and relevant information shared, doing only the things we like at the expense of things that really matter— and countless ways of wasting time.

> *Not urgent but important:* Paradoxically, the really important things are never urgent in the obvious sense. (It always

seems more urgent to return that telephone call than to set time aside for preparation and planning.) But, it is here that real leaders spend as much time as possible. This is where wise leaders meditate and think, where significant trends are discerned and relevant strategies formed, where goals are put into place and new thrusts are set in motion. In short, this is where leaders answer the question, "Where do I want to go?"

PRIORITIES: WHAT DO I NEED TO DO?

Once mission and aim are in place, it is a relatively simple matter to prioritize. Not only does this increase efficiency, but it also reinforces integrity. Decisions as to what to do and when to do it are made not in response to pressures of the moment but as expressions of the principles to which we are committed. Undoubtedly, leaders who live by a map find it easier to know what should be done. They can say "no" more readily and resist the distraction of other people's agendas; they organize weekly and know how to control their calendars. They find the balance between work and relaxation and are far more likely to be consistent leaders.

SCRUTINY: HOW AM I DOING?

The most careful travelers can find themselves going in the wrong direction. Anyone who enjoys the sport of orienteering will tell you how important it is to check your course frequently against the map and the compass. It is no different for leaders who try to live by a map. There must be time for regular and careful scrutiny of how we are doing.

- Are life and work heading in the direction we intend?

- Do our priorities truly reflect the principles to which we have committed ourselves?

- Are we resisting the demands of what is *urgent* while giving quality time to assessing what is really *important* in our lives?

A couple of hours spent reflecting on where we are and where we are headed can save months of wasted time and effort majoring in minors. Go back to the mission, read it quietly and carefully. Look at the aims and goals you have set for yourself. Reassess your priorities; you might have to affirm them again or even adjust them to take account of any changing circumstances. It will not be wasted effort, and it will ensure that you continue to be directed by the map rather than driven by the fleeting minutes.

Leaders Find a Mentor

Whenever I hear the *William Tell Overture* it reminds me of one of my childhood heroes—the Lone Ranger! The Cavendish Gang thought they had wiped out a six–man patrol of Texas Rangers. But one remained, John Reed, who took the name the Lone Ranger and wore a mask to conceal his identity as he embarked on his mission to rid the West of criminals such as the Cavendish Gang. Although he was the last of these Texas Rangers, he was not alone. He was smart enough to travel with his faithful companion Tonto, who came to his aid just at the right moment in every episode.

Many leaders talk about leadership being a lonely business—which it certainly is. But too many believe that it is an indication of weakness for a leader to seek help from someone else—which it certainly is not. We, too, need the support of a trusty companion, a mentor.

In one sense, anyone whom we admire and seek to emulate is a kind of mentor, although this is a somewhat passive interpretation of the relationship. There are those who fulfill the role of an occasional mentor—people such as teachers and tutors who impart their skills in specific situations. In its fullest sense, however, intentional mentoring takes place when an older, more mature individual agrees to accept a younger, less experienced person in a tutoring relationship in order to share skills and insights and to facilitate the growth of the younger person. The relationship of Paul and Timothy, for example, was obviously a mentoring one, and it provides us with a strong biblical foundation for the concept.

Those who want to be consistent leaders should seek a mentor. One of the greatest joys of my life over the last few years has been to fulfill the role of mentor for a young leader. We meet every couple of weeks and talk. Usually he sets the agenda, which arises from situations he is facing. Often he simply needs me to be a "sounding board" as he thinks aloud and works through his ideas. Occasionally, I pick a topic that I feel he needs to address. But it is not a one–way process. He asks me hard questions about my leadership; together, we hold the other mutually accountable. Not surprisingly, I think I have learned at least as much from him as he has from me. We help each other to be consistent leaders. I regret that I did not realize my need for a leadership mentor years ago; it would have helped me avoid many pitfalls. I am trying to make up for lost time, and I would strongly encourage every leader to both mentor and be mentored.

Leaders Follow the Master

In the end, if we are wise, we will turn our attention to the most consistent leader who ever lived—Jesus Christ. He is the perfect model for leadership as He is for everything else that truly matters in life. We will follow His life and deeds as they are revealed in Scripture, and we will draw on His love and power as we receive the Holy Spirit. An intimacy with Jesus is essential for authority in spiritual leadership. In their work titled *More Leadership Lessons of Jesus* (Broadman & Holman Publishers), writers Bob Briner and Ray Pritchard refer to Jesus as "a timeless model for today's leaders":

> When all the facts are fairly considered, we may safely say that Jesus Christ is the most effective leader the world has ever known. The tiny band He left behind has now become a worldwide fellowship numbering nearly two billion people in every nation on every continent. . . . Follow Jesus as He moves slowly toward His date with destiny in Jerusalem. Along the way you will discover how He took a group of very unlikely men and molded them into leaders who would carry on His work after He returned to heaven. . . . He is the Son of God and the greatest leader history has ever known.

six

Leading through Understanding

**One doesn't discover new lands without consenting
to lose sight of the shore for a very long time.**

André Gide, quoted in Peter Brierley, Vision Building

The question is often asked, Is a leader born or made? and the answer
has to be "yes" and "yes." If a man or woman does not have the leadership gift in some measure, then no amount of training will make him
or her a leader. It is also true to say that there have been many times in
history when circumstances have conspired to place seemingly unlikely
people in positions of leadership, where they have excelled to the surprise of everyone. To paraphrase the words of William Shakespeare,
some are born leaders, some achieve leadership, and some have leadership thrust upon them.

It is equally certain that not all leaders are the same. Different styles
and different approaches to leadership arise from various factors:

- the personality and abilities of the leader;
- the cultural context of the time and place;

- the area of human endeavor where leadership is exercised;
- the circumstances in which leadership is exercised; and
- the abilities and expectations of those being led.

It is often said that we need to find the style of leadership that is right for our personalities. But, given the variety of factors listed above, it is probably more helpful to think not of leadership styles but of leadership qualities, which need to be understood and applied in the right way, at the right time, and in the right situation. There is no such person as the perfect leader; some qualities of leadership will be met more easily than others because of our personalities, experiences, and abilities. Some might even be outside our area of competence. In that case, we will need to find colleagues who will work alongside us, complementing our strengths and weaknesses. As with many other things, leadership skills are best learned as we seek to put them into practice. Those who understand the main functions of leadership, however, will be in a better position to develop their skills than those who are simply "flying blind."

Leaders Establish Principles

This is the point at which character and competency intersect, the place where integrity links with strategy. Leaders establish principles—the non-negotiables of conviction and conduct that create trust in those who follow. Without them there can be no real leadership. Winston Churchill, Britain's great wartime leader, is a great illustration of this truth. It is often forgotten that for the first eight months of World War II Churchill was First Lord of the Admiralty and not prime minister. Historians have noted that his time in charge of the Royal Navy was undistinguished. And yet, when a crisis precipitated the resignation of Prime Minister Neville Chamberlain, it was to Churchill that the nation turned. The reason for his elevation to the highest office in the land is found in the years he spent out of office in the political wilderness.

Throughout that time, most British politicians favored a policy of appeasement toward Adolf Hitler and the Nazi regime. Churchill was a lone voice, one of the very few who saw the danger. He refused to compromise, although his views were unpalatable to the majority of his countrymen. In a steady stream of articles and pamphlets, he denounced the Nazi dictator and warned of his expansionist tendencies. He sternly counseled his countrymen, stating that they faced the "old grim choice—whether we shall submit or whether we shall prepare." When events proved Churchill to be right, he possessed a credibility in the eyes of his countrymen to which none of his fellow politicians could lay claim. The nation knew that here was the man to lead them through the dark days of war. Like all good leaders, he had established the principles which would govern his leadership and the direction he would ask his followers to go.

Leaders Define Purpose

The art of leadership has been described as taking people where they need to go and getting them to enjoy the journey. That being the case, a key task of a leader is to set the direction, and this is done by defining the purpose of the movement. Two questions must be addressed to help give clear direction to any organization existing to serve a sovereign God and a needy world.

WHAT IS OUR PRIMARY MOTIVATION?

Effective leaders know why God has brought a particular church or ministry into being. They also know how quickly and easily people can forget the very reason for their existence as an organization. Consequently, leaders will reiterate the founding vision of the movement, restating its roots in the very heart of God as revealed in Scripture. When The Christian Mission became The Salvation Army in 1878, William Booth defined for all time the God–given commission of this new movement:

> We are a salvation people—this is our specialty—getting saved and keeping saved, and then getting somebody else saved, and then getting saved ourselves more and more, until full salvation on earth makes the heaven within.

The primary motivation of The Salvation Army can never be changed without the organization becoming something very different. Of course, emphasis will shift within various aspects of its work and ministry, but its founding purpose is nonnegotiable. Subsequent leaders must remind us of that purpose and restate it for our times, as General John Gowans did more than 120 years after William Booth when he rallied Salvationists with a simple statement of our task: "To save souls, grow saints, and serve suffering humanity." The words may have been different, but the purpose remained the same. Were it otherwise, we would cease to be what we were called to be.

WHAT IS OUR CURRENT MISSION?

The overriding purpose of any movement is found in the work and will of God—the primary motivation. But that founding purpose must be lived out within the contexts of the present day and prevailing culture. Leaders must help their people discover their current mission, the way in which they fulfill their commitment to their purpose. Mission relates to the "here and now." It asks, What are the key objectives to fulfilling our purpose in contemporary society?

Because the context and conditions within which we work change, so will our mission. It is not something that will change every few months, but it may well have to change every five or ten years in response to the needs of a changing world. It will also vary somewhat in different parts of the world and in different parts within the same organization. Whereas the primary motivation illustrates our hearts pledged to God, the current mission expresses our hands stretched out to the world.

When we ask ourselves the "mission question," we are asking, in effect, What should we be doing at this particular time and place? At this point it is extremely useful to produce a mission statement, a simple but effective tool that helps keep us clearly focused on the work to be done. Three descriptions define a good mission statement:

> *Precise*—An effective mission statement needs to have precision of language, which provides clarity and distinction to the organization's purpose. The mission statement should answer the questions: Who are we? Who are the people we are trying to reach and serve? What is distinctive about us? What do we do well?

Concise—If a precise mission statement is to be useful, it needs to be short enough to be memorized without difficulty. So when you have answered the questions above, you then need to ask, What is really important, and what can be left out without diminishing the mission? It's amazing how much can be said in a few careful words, in a sentence which holds us to our shared calling and which we can easily recall and readily explain to others.

Visible—Concise mission statements with clear content need to be communicated in every way possible. They should be posted on notice boards, printed on stationery, and announced verbally as often as possible. Only then will the mission statement:

- help members of the organization focus on the essential work and ministry to which they have been called and avoid being side-tracked into activities which do not reflect their purpose;

- become the yardstick against which all other decisions— strategic, financial, organizational, and personnel—are tested;

- enable those outside the organization to understand its identity and ministry; and

- make it easier for members to be involved in collaborative initiatives with other groups. If members are sure of who they are and what they are doing, they will know not only what the group can contribute to a partnership, but also when a proposed partnership will be prejudicial to their best interests.

Leaders Cast the Vision

Vision is quite simply the presentation of the desired future, the powerful and inspiring picture of what we want to be and do. It doesn't lead to day-dreaming or fantasizing—far from it! Vision provides renewed energy for the task at hand today because it is vision that helps set a clear path through the present. Although vision has a future dimension, its power lies in the present. It becomes the dream that draws us onward, the light in the distance that gives us a sense of direction.

Vision must be anchored in present reality, but it must also reach out to future possibilities; it must be desirable but demanding; it must be firm enough to be a genuine target but flexible enough to be changed if circumstances alter; it must be precise enough to outline the route and daring enough to illustrate the desired results. Like a good mission statement, a vision is most powerful when it is distilled into a succinct and memorable sentence or two that can be shared with a passion and enthusiasm that will burn it into the hearts of everyone who hears it.

The powerful "I Have a Dream" speech articulated by Dr. Martin Luther King Jr. in Washington in 1963 is an unforgettable example of a leader casting the vision. To the 250,000 civil rights marchers who stood before him, King said:

> I have a dream that one day men will rise up and come to see that they are made to live together as brothers. I still have a dream this morning that one day every Negro in this country, every colored person in the world, will be judged on the basis of the content of his character rather than on the color of his skin, and every man will respect the dignity and worth of human personality.

His vision energized the civil rights movement to keep struggling for change and freedom from segregation. It provided inspiration for people to return to their communities and continue the hard and costly work of transforming the deeply ingrained prejudice of others. Such is the power of his vision that it still serves as a source of inspiration to thousands throughout the world working for justice and equality.

There is no doubt that some men and women are particularly gifted in this area of leadership. They are the visionaries with a God–given talent for inspiring their followers. But we must not allow our appreciation for their outstanding abilities to blind us to the fact that every leader needs to discover and cast a vision. As the Bible reminds us, "Where there is no vision, the people perish" (Proverbs 29:18 KJV).

Leaders cast the vision continually and creatively. They tell inspiring stories and speak in simple parables. They draw attractive word pictures in order to capture the hearts and imaginations of the people. Most of all, leaders seek to live by their vision, never giving into despondency, never settling for second best, always spilling passion and imparting enthusiasm. Instead of commanding others to do their duty, leaders call others to live the dream. Like Walt Whitman's traveler in "Song of the Open Road," leaders give themselves so that others will not so much follow as journey with them on an adventure of faith and love:

> Mon enfant! I give you my hand!
> I give you my love, more precious than money,
> I give you myself, before preaching or law;
> Will you give me yourself? will you come travel with me?
> Shall we stick by each other as long as we live?

Leaders Make an Impression

Not all leaders are extroverts. Nor are they all gifted in oratory. But all leaders have something about them that makes an impression—something that makes them stand out from the group yet also appeal to the group. There is something about leaders that makes people want to follow them. We are all familiar with the despotic tyrants of this world, who make an impression through displays of military hardware or by engineering a personality cult with their image projected for all to see. Such control over others runs contrary to the model of servant–leader to which we aspire. Jesus made an impression by His simplicity, His humility, and His topsy–turvy teaching, which told His listeners that in dying we live, in serving we achieve greatness, and in giving we receive. Making an impression does not depend primarily on extraordinary skill or power but on a display of humanity that combines authority with humility and strength with vulnerability.

Leaders Identify Priorities

A distinction should be made here between management and leadership. There is more than a little truth to the catchy phrase, "Management is about doing things right; leadership is about doing the right things." Organizations that are overmanaged and underled will tend to concentrate on maintenance of the status quo rather than on furthering the mission for which they exist. But this is not the whole truth. Management may not be identical to leadership, but it certainly is a component or adjunct of leadership.

A leader who does not possess management skills, or who does not have someone working alongside him with the necessary abilities in that area, may discover that the vision he has cast never comes to fruition. Indeed, the more inspiring the vision, the greater the frustration for those captivated by the picture set before them, those willing to give themselves to the cause of realizing the vision. Essentially, management is bringing everything into alignment with vision and purpose.

Good leaders identify priorities, imprint them in people's minds, and insist that this vision become the template for all that happens. Good leaders also don't control all the details. They will not micro-manage others or get bogged down in unnecessary detail, but they will make it their business to ensure that everything serves the vision. A prayer is displayed in my Manchester office that reads: "Lord, help us align our day-to-day work with the priorities You have given us." If that prayer is not constantly made by my staff, then we may be busy but we will ultimately be unproductive. The task of leadership is to make sure that never happens!

Leaders Develop People

All true leadership has a dual purpose—to achieve the agreed-upon goals and to develop the people who have committed themselves to the task. Even some great leaders have failed at this point, and often their failure is not noticed until the leader leaves office and there is a leadership vacuum. No one is ready to take over. No effort has been given to the development of people and the nurturing of leaders. In *Courageous Leadership*, Bill Hybels emphasizes the necessary investment of time and energy that is needed in this aspect of leadership:

In order for emerging leaders to become seasoned, wise, and effective leaders, they need proximity to and interaction with veteran leaders. . . . In Jesus' day it was common for leaders–in–training to simply follow the veteran leader around. They would talk together, walk together, eat their meals together, sleep in neighboring tents. They would spend months, some-times years, apprenticing. This allowed them to internalize the vision and values of the veteran leader in ways that served them the rest of their lives. . . . I'm not sure a better approach has been discovered in the centuries since then.

More than anything else in all the world, the Christian gospel brings together the call to a great cause—the establishment of God's kingdom on earth—with the challenge to develop people to their fullest potential as effective disciples of Jesus Christ. True leaders will never regard people as an irritating distraction. Rather, they will see them as men and women in whom the image of God must be restored; to whom time, effort, and care must be freely given; and through whom the purposes of God will be achieved.

seven

Leading a Team

Jesus went up on a mountainside
and called to Him those He wanted, and they came to Him.
He appointed twelve—designating them
apostles—that they might be with Him and that He might send
them out to preach and to have authority to drive out demons.

Mark 3:13–15

The essence of leadership is not found in lonely isolation or in spectacular inspiration of the masses but in creating a team of people who will share the vision and carry the work forward. No leader, however gifted, can achieve lasting success on his or her own. When leaders share their beliefs with a tightly knit group of followers, they themselves become leaders.

The existence of the Christian Church is proof of the effectiveness of such team building. Jesus Christ established His Church and ensured the future of His mission by investing Himself in and entrusting His work to His little band of disciples. He knew how to stand alone, He could hold a crowd spellbound, but He ultimately risked the entire success of His mission on twelve very ordinary men. And within a relatively few years, they began to turn the world on its head with their extraordinary power.

Six Aspects of Effective Teams

Christian leaders should need no persuading that building and leading a team is the formula for maximum success. It is by no means an easy route to take, but there are skills that can be understood, learned, and put into practice which will enable us to follow the example of our Servant–Master.

THE UNDERLYING PRINCIPLE

Building and working with a team does not make life easier. In fact, the opposite is often true. Teams take time, partnership requires patience, and cooperation is hard work. It is often easier and quicker—at least in the short term—to do things yourself. So why form a team? The answer is simple: Teamwork allows us to achieve a level of excellence that would otherwise be quite impossible. When a team is functioning well, a synergy is released that can be breathtaking.

Wherever there is a need to get things done or to provide ongoing and comprehensive direction of any project or organization, there is a need for a team. Some teams will have a limited lifespan, such as a team set up to drive a specific fundraising project. Other teams, such as the leadership team of a church or the board of directors of a large corporation, will exist as long as the larger body remains. They can vary in size, but the most effective teams rarely exceed a dozen members. If they are any larger, they become inefficient and need to be divided into subgroups. Each subgroup then becomes a team in itself, with the leaders of each subgroup forming a leadership team.

Not every group of people who work together deserves to be called a team. There has to be intentionality, a "buy in," a willingness to work together. My personal definition of a team owes as much to my reading and listening to others as to my own thought and experience:

> A real and effective team is a group of interdependent people, committed to an agreed purpose and to an acknowledged

leader, who freely choose to work together and cooperate to achieve that purpose, to reach a level of excellence that would otherwise be impossible, and to allow and assist each member to achieve his or her greatest potential in the achievement of that purpose.

THE INDISPENSABLE PRAYER

When Luke relates the story of Jesus' choosing His disciples, He includes a significant detail:

> One of those days Jesus went out to a mountainside to pray, and spent the night praying to God. When morning came He called His disciples to Him and chose twelve of them whom He also designated apostles. (Luke 6:12,13)

Before Jesus selected His inner circle of the twelve, He spent an entire night in prayer. Effective teams require an enormous amount of prayer, not only in selecting the team but also regarding the ongoing relationships of its members. When a group of people work closely together, a great deal of grace and patience is required on all sides. A team is a microcosm of the whole Church—the body of Christ in miniature—and prayer is the vital channel through which divine power and guidance flow. Specific and regular periods of prayer are necessary when meeting to worship together. Apart from the spiritual dynamic they release, they also play a great part in bonding the team. "Emergency" prayer can be equally powerful in breaking down barriers when relationships are strained or when a seemingly insurmountable problem needs to be faced. One of the leader's primary functions, as he seeks direction regarding membership, motivation, and mission of his team, is to put time aside for prayer, for listening to all that God is saying. Leaders must never be so absorbed with the practicalities of leadership that they forget the importance of prayer.

THE OBVIOUS PRIORITY

It is highly significant that, after telling us of Jesus' call of the twelve, the gospel writers go on to list their names. I am certain that this is more than just a point of information, a "Who's who" in the band of disciples.

What we are meant to understand is that these may have been very ordinary men, but they were chosen men. They were not there by accident or happenstance; they were there because Jesus wanted them on His team. Identifying them and calling them to His side was one of the priorities of His earthly ministry. To others they would have appeared unremarkable; to Jesus they were special, unique, and vital to the completion of His mission.

It is both a privilege and an enormous responsibility when we choose the team with whom we work, and the process of choosing is worth giving all the time and care available. When we bring people onto our team, we combine prayer, interview, references, spiritual gift identification, and personality profiling. Not only do we ask ourselves, Can this person do the job we need done? but we also wonder, Can he or she fit in with our team *ethos* and become passionate about our mission? The most gifted person in the world is no use to us if he or she disrupts the fellowship which lies at the heart of all we do. I remind team members that it is better to be one person short than to panic and employ the wrong person.

Of course, it is not always possible to choose our team. Often we are appointed to a position where the team already exists: They did not choose us and we did not choose them. What must happen, however, is that the choice still needs to be made. As stated before, there has to be an openness and a willingness to work together. The leader has to find ways of saying to the team, "I may have been appointed to you, but I am gladly embracing you as my team." Much time spent on one–on–one conversations and team–building exercises will prove invaluable. Perhaps like the arranged marriages I have encountered among colleagues and friends from other cultures, the choice of partner may have been made by the "parents," but the "couple" must learn to embrace each other, creating a marriage that is strong and vibrant and resilient!

The motivating purpose

If it is true that there is nothing more unmotivating for an individual than the lack of a clear and definite purpose, it is equally true for a team. Successful teams are driven by a purpose that is worth the lives offered in service by its members. No one knew this better than Jesus:

> Jesus went into Galilee, proclaiming the good news of God. "The time has come," He said. "The kingdom of God is near. Repent and believe the good news!" As Jesus walked beside the Sea of Galilee, He saw Simon and his brother Andrew casting a net into the lake, for they were fishermen. "Come, follow Me," Jesus said, "and I will make you fishers of men." At once they left their nets and followed Him. (Mark 1:14–18)

In these few short, dramatic sentences we can discover all we need to know about a purpose that will motivate a team.

Team members need to be inspired

When Jesus appeared on the scene at the beginning of His ministry, He came with good news—the kingdom of God was breaking through. To a people oppressed by an occupying army and longing to hear again the authentic voice of God that had once sounded so clearly through the prophets, that must have been exciting news indeed. At long last, here was hope in an otherwise hopeless world. The message of the kingdom was an inspiration in an almost literal sense. It breathed new life into those who heard and responded.

People still need to be inspired. On July 13, 1985, the rock musician Bob Geldof inspired an entire generation to take notice of the famine crisis in Africa and offer assistance through "Live Aid." This sixteen–hour concert was attended by more than 70,000 people and watched by 1.4 billion television viewers in over 150 countries. Nearly $100 million was raised for famine relief—the most money ever raised for charity by a single event—and used to fund projects in Mozambique, Chad, Burkina Faso, Niger, Mali, the Sudan, and Ethiopia. Geldof was an artist, not a promoter, with no previous experience managing such an enormous project. But he made the whole thing happen by his inspirational insistence that something should be done and could be done. It was no easy task, costing him dearly in physical and emotional energy. In his book *Is That It?* (Weidenfeld & Nicolson), Geldof writes:

> It was the need to be able to encourage others, to always say, Of course it's possible," that drained me. . . . I was scared at

night in bed; quite literally, I lay in a bath of cold sweat. I would wake up after being asleep for an hour, scared beyond reason. Imagine failing. Imagine failure on such a scale.

The project may not be so large and the prospect not nearly so daunting, but every leader worthy of the name will learn to pay the price of inspiring others with a purpose that is worthy of great effort.

Team members need to be compelled

The message that Jesus brought was more than just an announcement of the good news of the kingdom of God; it was also a compelling call to become part of that kingdom and to share in its work. Inspiration must lead to a captivating invitation to get involved. Any worthwhile purpose "grabs" the listener. The words of Jesus, "Come, follow Me," were to change the lives of those humble fishermen forever. They also ring through the centuries, taking hold of the hearts and minds of countless millions who have been arrested by the greatest purpose of all.

Great leaders have a gift for making others feel important and needed and for communicating a message with an intensely personal impact. Effective teams are composed of individuals who have been challenged by their leader, who have been captivated by the mission, and who are convinced that they can help get the job done.

Team members need to be employed

"Follow me," said Jesus, "and I will make you fishers of men." It is not enough to offer inspiration and to engage the commitment of team members. They must be set to work, employed in labor that is both meaningful and satisfying. That was part of the genius of William Booth. The writer Cyril Barnes spoke of Booth's practical Christianity in the book *Words of William Booth* when he commented on Booth's instruction to his son, Bramwell, to "go and do something" for the homeless of London:

> William Booth was not only a theorist; he was a do-er. In turn he wanted no idle soldiers; he wanted workers. And he wanted to see initiative.

Few things erode motivation more than the sense of being under-employed. One of the most important tasks of a leader is to ensure that everyone within the team is suitably employed, that their work matches their capacity and ability, and that encouragement and appreciation are generously given at every opportunity.

Team members need to be extended

I often tell people that the highest compliment ever paid to me was from one of my daughters. I was encouraging her in her studies and telling her how well she was doing and that I thought she had the ability to do even better. It was then that she said, "Dad, maybe I'm not as good as you think I am." My response was immediate and insistent. "Of course you are. In fact, I think you're probably even better than that!" The expression on her face at that moment left me in no doubt that she believed me enough to try and prove me correct.

The principle applies as much to teams as to families. People respond best and do their best work when encouraged to move out of their comfort zone, beyond the boundaries of what they previously believed to be their limitations. The literal translation of the original Greek in Mark's account of the call of the disciples is: "I will make you to become fishers of men." The disciples would not only change the world; they themselves would be changed. As they followed Jesus, they would be undergoing a process of becoming.

Being part of any genuine team involves the challenge and responsibility of becoming, of developing. Therefore, every leader should seek to delegate not only in order to achieve the end in view but also to develop the individual. However, unless the leader gives the right kind of support, the team member can be left to flounder, damaging the confidence of the individual and the effectiveness of the team.

THE ENABLING CAPTAIN

The task of a ship's captain is not just to sail in the designated direction, but to return safely to harbor; it is to ensure that the ship reaches its precise destination and then berths in exactly the right place. A team needs a leader who fulfills such a function, constantly checking the direction and speed at which things are moving, watching out for the hazards that can knock them off course or even do lasting damage to the stability of the group. The team leader who is an able captain will devote time and effort to the following tasks.

Clarity

It's amazing how often people who work in a group have no concrete idea of what the group is trying to do or how their role is meant to contribute to the desired outcome. A team captain constantly clarifies what the goal is and what people need to do to reach that goal. Using words that engage the imagination, a team leader brings clarity in such a way that people—far from feeling threatened—understand how they can move from where they are to where they need to be. When Jesus called the fishermen by the Sea of Galilee, He called them to become "fishers of men." That was a concept they could understand, even if the deeper implications of the words were still to be worked out in their lives. They could begin to see what Jesus was about and the part they had to play.

Clarity is the foundation on which the compatibility of the individual to their assigned role is built. The leader will constantly assess the character, commitment, and competence of each person within the team and ask if they are right for the assigned task. Sometimes the task will need to be adjusted, sometimes people will need to be challenged as to their commitment, sometimes their lack of competence will require further training or re-assignment within the team, and sometimes leaders have to do the painful job of dealing with character issues. These are the aspects of leadership which cannot be avoided if the team is to be kept on track and the members are to be held accountable for their actions.

Confidence

Clarity and compatibility inevitably lead to confidence. People who know they're in the right seat, on the right train, with the right driver, going in the right direction, and heading for the right destination, rarely jump off, even if the line is occasionally a little bumpy! They may even enjoy the journey and appreciate the scenery. The same thing happens in a well-led team. It may be hard work, but it sure is fun; it may be demanding, but it's definitely worth the effort.

A team leader supports his individual members as he seeks to extend and develop them by delegating increasing responsibility. If such delegation happens too slowly, team members become frustrated; if it is done too quickly and without the right level of supervision, they are likely to fail. A good leader understands the art of measured delegation and appropriate supervision. To visualize the process, picture the following four stages of delegation:

Holding hands—

When I was about nine or ten years old my dad decided to teach me how to play golf. To say that I was not a natural golfer is to seriously understate my lack of natural ability at the game. But my dad never got annoyed and never gave up on me. Instead, as I held the golf club, he would stand behind me, wrap his arms around me, and take my hands in his. Together we would swing the driver, and the results always amazed me. Left to myself I either missed the ball completely or sent it flying in any direction but that which I intended. When Dad and I swung together, the ball flew straight and true. Gradually my confidence grew, and I began to do what had previously been impossible for me.

Often we are asked to perform tasks for which we have neither natural aptitude nor suitable experience. Left alone, we fail abysmally. But if we are supervised closely, shown how to do the task, and assisted as we do it, we slowly, surely develop both confidence and ability. There is no shame in admitting we don't know how to do something. Far from indicating failure, it is the first step to success. Failure occurs only when we don't speak up or when the leader or other team members neglect to help.

When a team member is inexperienced or very nervous about carrying out a task, holding hands—direct and close supervision—is the most appropriate leadership style.

Standing back—

Despite my dad's best efforts, I never did become proficient at golf. Riding a bicycle, however, was quite another thing. I wanted to do that more than anything else when I was a kid. It seemed to me that there was nothing more liberating and grown up than riding a couple of streets to a friend's house. Recognizing that I had a reasonable sense of balance and a real determination to succeed, my dad used a different style and level of supervision. Once I was settled on the bicycle, he would run behind me, keeping his hands on the back of the seat just enough to give me a little extra support. Then, when he thought I was balanced, he would take his hands off, stand back, and let me ride. Sure, I fell off a couple of times, but I still remember the thrill of riding free and the joy of realizing that I was doing it on my own.

In standing back, my dad was demonstrating another useful style of leadership. We worked together just long enough for me to gain the necessary confidence, but as soon as possible he let me go on my own. Of course, he stayed close by to help me if I fell off or to warn me if I disobeyed the rules of the road. This is the same kind of behavior we employ when we explain to someone the task that needs to be done, offer some basic guidance or a brief demonstration, give them the chance to ask questions and seek clarification, and then let them take over with the knowledge that we are available to assist if they need us.

This style of leadership gives a team member, especially someone who clearly has enthusiasm or aptitude for a task, the independence that allows him or her to work with dignity and competency. It also allows the team leader to move beyond supervision that is direct and close to a kind of support that is a more distant and discreet.

Handing over—

Learning to drive was, for me, a little different than learning to play golf or ride a bicycle. My instructors guided me through the first two stages of delegation, where they supervised and supported me as I began to master the basic skills. But the day came when the keys were handed over to me, and I was invited to go through all the necessary procedures and make all the relevant decisions as I drove the car into town. My friend, who was an experienced driver, sat beside me but said nothing apart from making casual conversation. Only when we had reached our destination and I had switched off the engine did we discuss my driving. It was not until later, as I reflected on the experience, that I appreciated the fact that my friend had been willing to risk his life on my competence as a driver. I felt rather proud of my efforts and very grateful for his trust!

The leadership style of handing over is always risky, but it is vital if a leader is to allow his team to gain confidence and develop to their fullest capacity. There is no higher compliment a leader can pay his team members than to take a risk on them. There must be opportunity for evaluation and feedback, for constructive criticism and self-assessment; but the task to be done has to be left essentially to the novice. If a leader never allows his team to reach this stage he will trap them in dependency, and he will have failed to bring them to their full potential.

Pushing out—

I have learned to play golf, ride a bicycle, and drive a car. However, I must confess to one, as yet, unfulfilled ambition: I want one day to parachute jump solo! I can only imagine the thrill of leaping from the airplane, floating through sky, feeling the air rush past my face, and then landing safely on solid ground. Of course, to reach that point, I would have to be guided through the stages listed above. But one day, the moment of fear and exhilaration would arrive—the biggest adrenaline rush of all time—I would be ready to be "pushed out" of the plane.

That's the greatest point to which a leader can bring his team: Once he has taught them all he can, once he has held their hands, stood back a little, and handed over a number of tasks to them, there comes a time to "push them out"—to delegate to them total responsibility for making and implementing decisions in a specified area. The most important work a leader can do is help his team become leaders in their own right. Sometimes they will fail, but more often they will surprise themselves by achieving a level of excellence never before thought possible. A true leader will enjoy that moment more than anything else in the world.

THE ESSENTIAL PROCESSES

If you want to know how people are likely to cope in a given situation, it is often wise to take a look at their record, at how they have worked and performed in the past. It is the same with a team as with an individual. The way a team has worked in the past gives a clear indication of how it is likely to do in the future. The record reveals the level of emotional health and practical efficiency of a team, and to the extent that these attributes are measured depends considerably on the essential processes of a team. In fact, we can outline these processes by using the word *record:*

Relationships

Leaders are obsessed with relationships. They know that if relationships are good, almost any difficulty can be overcome. Equally, if relationships are bad, the smallest difficulty can become an insurmountable obstacle. Consequently, leaders spend a lot of their time fostering good relationships within their team. They model healthy attitudes; they find time to talk with members; they insist on courtesy while allowing differing opinions to be heard; they insist that conflicts are resolved and that hurts are never left to fester; they take every opportunity to thank people for tasks well done. In addition, leaders never allow sulking or gossip in the team; they never tolerate disruptive people who refuse to listen to reason or insist on plowing their own furrow regardless of the priorities of the team; and they do everything in their power to combat divisiveness and dissension. Quality relationships is the glue that holds teams together.

Equilibrium

An underestimated art of team leadership is the ability to maintain proper equilibrium, allowing individual members to achieve the right balance between focusing on their own specified tasks and being fully involved in the team. Leaders recognize that their team members serve a dual function: to specialize in a particular area of service (i.e., evangelism, social service, youth work, finance) and to represent a multi–disciplinary team. In strategy discussions, the financial director should be as free to speak on mission as on finance, and the youth director should be as welcome to give an opinion on finance as on the subject of ministry to young people. It never ceases to amaze me how insightful people can be outside their own discipline and how much synergy is released when the team tackles issues as a group. Of course, the leader needs to control any over-stepping into someone else's area of responsibility or any negligence of one's own tasks. But with careful handling, a proper and productive equilibrium can be maintained.

Communication

By providing accessible and effective pathways of communication so that their team always knows what is happening, leaders keep creativity flowing and common purposes fresh. However this is done—at formal meetings (to ensure that everyone hears the same thing at the same time), through clear, concise emails or memos, during more casual gatherings or one-on-one encounters, where conversation takes place in a relaxed manner—it is a crucial priority. Inadequate leaders regard inquiries from team members as inconvenient interruptions; good leaders regard inquiries as priceless opportunities for quality communication. They practice management by leaving the door open.

Order

Informal communication is very different, however, from anarchy and chaos. Teams can only work well when there is a high degree of order. Contrary to a multitude of rules and regulations, good order is unobtrusive and can usually be distilled into a few clear principles. Courtesy, clarity, accuracy, and brevity are the watchwords of highly effective teams. Formal meetings must start punctually, be as brief as is practically possible, and produce minutes which are timely and accurate. Disagreements are honestly faced, resolved as far as possible, and never aired in a manner that is personal or offensive. When discipline has to be administered it is done privately and is designed to correct rather than punish. Above all, everyone on the team is clear about what the primary task is. As the saying goes, the main thing is to keep the main thing the main thing. Good order serves the purpose of clear focus, and clear focus makes sure that everyone is heading in the same direction.

Review

A characteristic of insecure leaders is their unwillingness to allow team members to question the way things are done. Secure, confident leaders, on the other hand, encourage regular review processes from the team. They know that others often have insights and perspectives that can lead to better methods and more efficient practices. Reviews give the team—and the leader—an opportunity to assess overall effectiveness, critique policy, and evaluate progress. Indeed, good leaders will even seek constructive criticism from outside the team, from the people whom they exist to serve. An old gospel song includes the words,

> I'm not what I ought to be, but
> I'm better than I used to be, and
> I'm getting better all the time!

Leaders who can say that of themselves and their team may be far from perfection, but they are certainly on the right track to excellence.

Decision making

It may appear to be stating the obvious, but good teams make decisions that lead to action. The best–led discussions, the most innovative ideas, the most carefully thought out plans mean nothing unless things actually get done! That is why strategy is addressed in the next chapter.

eight

Leading with Strategy

Leadership is the capacity to translate vision into reality.

Warren G. Bennis, quoted in John C. Maxwell, One Minute Leadership

God did not simply dream of a beautiful world of plants and animals populated by human creatures made in His image. He created it stage by stage, making sure at the end of each day that what He had made was good. The hand of God painstakingly created what the heart of God had lovingly conceived. In other words, a leader's vision must be translated into reality. If that does not happen, people will be left disillusioned and frustrated, like a man who can see the glorious snow–peaked mountains through the bars of the dismal dungeon in which he is trapped. Inspiration alone is not enough. If there is to be any transformation and lasting satisfaction, it needs to be followed by a great deal of preparation and perspiration. Casting the vision, a primary function of leadership, is only a step on a leader's journey to the realization of his mission. As the heart and head must work together, vision must be closely linked to strategy.

Strategy of Investigation

First, there are things we need to find out: Where are we starting from as we set out to achieve the realization of our mission? What is the true picture of the world in which we have to work and minister? What is the true picture of our organization?

EXTERNAL ANALYSIS

Few things are more disheartening than the decline of a church or organization that once served the needs of its people well but failed to adapt to a changed world. The good news of God's love through Jesus never changes—nor does the world's need of a Savior. Yet the way in which that need presents itself constantly does change, and the methods to communicate and deliver the grace of God should change as well.

To develop a relevant strategy we need to ask some simple but vital questions:

- What are the needs of the people we seek to serve?
- Do these people participate in our programs and services?
- Have we ever asked them what they think?
- What changes—social, demographic, and cultural—have taken place in our community and in society at large in the last five, ten, twenty years?
- How has technology changed? How does that affect the way we do things?
- What future trends can we detect? How will they affect what we are doing?

These questions can be addressed, at least in part, within a leadership team discussion. Perhaps a house-to-house survey, using a carefully prepared questionnaire, could offer some important insights. Government census reports also provide a wealth of demographic information. If finances allow, research can be commissioned from a competent and trusted resource. Finally, reading about changes in our society can help us detect trends that influence us today. It will take time and effort, but if we don't know where we are starting, we are unlikely to get where we think we are going!

Internal analysis

The Scottish poet Robert Burns once wrote:

O wad some Power the giftie gie us
To see oursels as ithers see us!
It wad frae mony a blunder free us,
An' foolish notion.

In other words, if we could only see ourselves objectively, we would avoid many of our mistakes. Again, the secret is to ask the right questions:

- How relevant is our contribution to the community?

- What results are achieved by our presence and programs?

- What should be our response to the changes in society and the needs which arise out of those changes?

- What resources do we have—people, finance, facilities, equipment—to improve what we are doing or to start something new?

- Is our contribution part of our stated mission, or is there an unspoken internal culture with differing values? (This is often the hardest question to answer honestly!)

If Robert Burns is correct, we are not always in the best position to assess our own performance. It is often helpful, therefore, to ask others for an objective perspective using similar questions. We can ask the opinions of consultants, of those we are trying to serve, even of our members. However we do it, an "internal audit" is an essential step to real progress.

Strategy of Decision

Someone once complained to Billy Graham, "I don't like the way you do evangelism." His reply was characteristically direct: "Well, I prefer the way I do it to the way you don't do it!" Dr. Graham's point is one we must heed. There's way too much talking and philosophizing and not nearly enough doing in the world. All our investigating and analysis is worthless if we don't come to a point of decision. The hard reality is that we cannot do everything. Some things are not in our genetic makeup; we were never created to do them. Other things we might like to do, but we have to accept that we have limited resources. This is the point at which we need to combine realism with an element of risk. The wisdom to give careful consideration to the facts must be counter–balanced by the willingness to step out in faith. Hard, clear thinking must stand alongside fervent, obedient prayer. Ask, "What is God saying to us?"

STRATEGIC THRUSTS

A good strategy needs a few thrusts—general directions in which we want to go. I can best illustrate what I mean by referring to a recent experience when my own team went through this exercise relating to the work of The Salvation Army in the northwest section of England. Our vision was clear and simple: to reposition the Army as an effective force for evangelism and mission in a community that has changed almost beyond recognition in the past twenty years.

Our external investigation revealed a picture of rapidly declining church attendance, a breakdown of family life and traditional values, an increasing gap between rich and poor, a fear of crime—but also a deep and genuine spiritual longing allied by an unprecedented willingness of statutory authorities to work with faith–based groups. Our internal audit presented us with the hard reality of an aging and declining membership in some areas, a number of buildings reaching the end of their usefulness, and a growing gulf between the cultures of our traditions and those of our communities. On the other hand, there were real evidences of growth in certain areas. Our social services were greatly respected, we had a nucleus of gifted young leaders, and the Army had an influence and reputation far greater than our size would lead one to expect. So we settled on a number of strategic thrusts.

- Increasing our commitment to prayer
- Planting new congregations
- Placing a stronger emphasis on youth work

- Directing our limited resources to those congregations of greatest potential for growth and outreach

- Continuing to raise the standards of our social and community services

- Giving greater importance to evangelism and discipleship

- Speaking and working for social justice

Strategy of Action

As investigation needs to lead to decision, decision must lead to action. Identifying strategic thrusts provides the impetus for that action: How are we going to do it? When are we going to do it? Who is going to be responsible for doing it? The next step is to translate them into *smart* goals—clear targets that are:

- *S*pecific
- *M*easurable
- *A*chievable
- *R*ealistic
- *T*ime-based

It is essential to remember two things—priority and responsibility. Everything cannot be done at once, so decide what is most important, what must be done first, and who leads each task. The following list of goals arose from our example of the strategic thrusts. They specify both the objective and assigned leader:

- Create a prayer room and establish three daily fifteen-minute prayer times for the leadership team within the next two months—*divisional leader*

- Plant one new congregation each year for the next five years—*director of evangelism*

- "Pump prime" six existing congregations by allocating additional resources over the next five years for extra full-time staff—*director of finance and director of evangelism*

- Recruit young people into youth cells and provide them with culturally relevant worship, mission opportunities, and social action projects within the next three years— *youth officer*

Strategy of Communication

Too often, the best laid plans go wrong for no other reason than we didn't tell anyone! Communication is a vital aspect of strategy development. It's a little bit like leading a party up a misty mountain. If you forget to check that everyone is accounted for and knows where to go, someone will get lost—with possibly disastrous consequences. To keep a team focused on the mission, there needs to be a plan that constantly and creatively reminds the group where they are heading.

Our team decided on a logo with a simple slogan—shape the future through prayer—which we now feature on all our publicity. The word *prayer* also serves as a useful acrostic on which to hang the main points of our strategic direction:

- *P*lant new congregations
- *R*each out through effective social and community services
- *A*rmy on the frontline
- *Y*outh emphasis
- *E*nhance and encourage mission initiatives
- *R*adical discipleship and evangelism

Both the slogan and acrostic have been printed on posters and wallet-sized laminated cards to remind others of the strategic direction. When members of the divisional leadership team conduct the Sunday worship in any of our centers, "Shape the future through prayer" is featured in our worship and preaching. This is not the only way to communicate, of course, but it is just one example of trying to keep the message at the forefront of everyone's mind.

Strategy of Evaluation

One thing is certain regarding our own experience of strategic planning—it won't work out exactly as we have planned! Time will tell, I'm sure, that we were plain wrong about some things. Other ideas might have been right when we started out, but as circumstances and personnel change, the strategy may need to be adjusted and refined. That's why regular evaluation is essential. It calls for trust and integrity from those who are involved, but it is worth the effort. An effective evaluation is based on the following four-step process:

> *Gather the information.* How does our progress stack up against our original goals? Is there anything that is simply not working out? Have the responsibilities been allocated correctly? Do new challenges or opportunities exist which were previously unknown?
>
> *Assess the implications.* What does this information mean for us? What do we need to change? Is there anything we need to abandon? Do any of the projects need increased resources? Are the difficulties we face the result of opposition, insufficient application, or just the inevitable setbacks of the real world?
>
> *Adjust the direction.* Where do we need to alter or fine-tune the strategy? Is God closing a door to us and telling us to take a different approach?
>
> *Renew our dedication.* Are we still doing what God wants? Is He saying anything new to us?

Objections may arise that such careful strategic planning has little or no place in the Christian Church, that we should simply leave it to God. But that is not the case, and it certainly wasn't the case in the early church. Careful reading of the Acts of the Apostles reveals that the early

Christians engaged in an enormous amount of prayer allied with a high level of planning and organizing as they faced the challenges of mission in a hostile world. We will need that same combination if we are to emulate their success in sharing the gospel.

Clichés may be trite, but they are sometimes true. May we never be guilty of either of the following:

> People who fail to pray, are prey to failure.
> People who fail to plan, plan to fail.

nine

Leading Change

Imagine a church in twenty–first century America or Europe where the services are conducted in the language of Chaucer, where the congregation wears medieval dress, where the music has not changed since the fifteenth century, where the members refuse to install electricity—and where the leaders defend their unwillingness to change as loyalty to the unchanging gospel! The idea is ridiculous, of course, but it is only an extreme example of a conservatism so often afflicting Christian churches. It is all too easy for us to cling to the past, to insist on doing things that no longer work in today's world, and to justify our stubbornness as an expression of our faithfulness.

In his book *Prepare Your Church for the Future* (Fleming H. Revell), Carl George summarized, over a decade ago, the seriousness of the challenge facing the church. The ensuing years have simply served to underline the truth of his words:

> Churches are faced with a . . . dilemma. We quickly forget that the felt needs of our "customers" are in a constant state of flux. We can overlook the fact that each new day ushers in a slightly different set of circumstances. We sometimes neglect the long-range implications of not keeping abreast with the present. Instead, we often persevere in the comfortable habits to which we've grown accustomed. . . . Are we willing to face the reality that people, even spiritually hungry individuals, are passing us by as they walk down the street of life? . . . We need to take a fresh look at what God has called us to be. We need a new way of measuring our health and effectiveness. And we need a readiness to induce changes that are needed. I believe that the choices challenging Christians today are so great that, for many local churches, their very existence is, or will soon be, at stake.

Change is here to stay! Effective spiritual leaders in the twenty-first century will need to lead and manage change. If change doesn't happen, the church will become increasingly irrelevant and out of touch. If it happens too quickly, or if it is badly managed, the results could be disastrous, with leaders chasing every passing phase or following every new trend while having no real sense of purpose or direction. Leading change is never easy. It is painful and costly for all concerned, but it can also be liberating and exciting when it is managed well. What follows are the tasks and skills required for leading change.

Facing Reality

Churches and organizations can become so wrapped up in what they are doing that they never stop to ask how effective their work is. And the less effective something is, the harder they work at it. This kind of perverted sense of commitment is a particularly hazardous temptation for Christian organizations. As a colleague once expressed it, "We've sanctified sterility and called it faithfulness." Meaningful change begins only when we are ready to face reality and recognize our ineffectiveness. Then we who have veered off the road of failure can steer onto the road of success.

Generating Urgency

Change can happen only when there is a sense of urgency, when people realize that the status quo is not an option and the consequences of failure are fully understood. In order to generate such an urgency, leaders need to overcome two equal and opposite dangers:

COMPLACENCY

The same phrases are heard again and again when people talk about the need for change. "Yes," they say, "there are problems," Then there follows a whole series of "buts": "Things are not as bad as they seem." "No one else is doing any better than we are, and we know some who are doing a lot worse." "Other churches are growing because they've deserted the truth and they're just crowd pleasers." "The world has gone wrong, and we're the remnant holding onto the pure gospel." The list of excuses could fill a book, yet the reasons behind such complacency are not difficult to discern:

- An impending crisis may not be obvious to everyone. But a crisis that is not immediately obvious is no less real.

- Often people gauge success by the wrong yardstick—measuring the success of their church, for example, by its mere survival, its financial stability, or by the fact that its congregation is happy and comfortable.

- Human beings have a limitless capacity for denial. This is sometimes seen as a tendency to "talk things up," making everything seem better than it really is; or it may manifest as a "kill the messenger" attitude, where criticism of any kind is viewed as disloyalty.

- Many churches and organizations receive very little feedback from the people they exist to serve. Consequently, they are unable to make an objective assessment of their standing in the wider community.

- If a church belongs to a denomination where resources of money and manpower are fed in from external sources, the people can easily be blinded to the true state of affairs. For example, congregations who receive income from a trust fund or from central denominational finances can be oblivious to the fact that its members are failing to tithe.

Several measures may be necessary to generate the sense of urgency that will overcome such complacency and alert people to the need for change:

- *Looking at hard statistics* provides indisputable evidence of decline. A sleepy congregation can look at a carefully prepared graph showing trends over a ten-year period and feel the effect of being drenched with cold water!

- *Asking for constructive criticism* from trusted outsiders brings a much-needed dose of objectivity to those in denial. Professional consultants are useful, as are sympathetic but honest friends willing to confront us with any unpalatable truths.

- *Observing quality work* at other successful ministries is a useful tool by which to measure our own efforts.

- *Replacing cautious management* with daring, innovative leadership is crucial. Careful stewardship must give way to a spirit of bold pioneering. Permission to make mistakes and try something new must be given.

- *Measuring everything against the primary motivation,* the greater purpose in all we do—this is the secret above all else to overcoming complacency. Every church that measures itself against their God-given commission will be jolted out of complacency and confronted with the need to change.

Despondency

At the opposite end of the scale from complacency is despondency. Those in its grip have an equally long litany of laments explaining why change will never work: "The world is in a terrible state, and things will only get worse." "We've tried it all before but nothing works." "We're willing to try something new, but there's too much opposition from the traditionalists." "We would like to change, but we don't have the skills."

It takes time, effort, and enormous energy, but despondency can be overcome with a combination of enthusiastic leadership, effective and innovative training, and exciting victories which demonstrate that change is possible, beneficial, and enjoyable. Of course, not everyone will get on board quickly or easily, but the leader who can create a sense of urgency will eventually turn around even the most conservative group.

Releasing Synergy

Imagine the amount of energy required to start a stationery train and get it moving up to full speed in the right direction. Leading change requires an input of emotional, intellectual, and spiritual energy no less great! A single individual, however gifted and passionate, cannot lead such change on his own. If he tries, he will either reach a point of emotional meltdown or realize that his progress goes no further than his immediate associates and no deeper than a cosmetic change. What is needed is not just energy, but synergy—the dynamism that is released when people work together for a common goal. For synergy to occur, two things are needed.

A team that is committed

A committed team will have the single-minded drive required for deep and lasting change. It is not formed by simply selecting a random group of people; it must include key people—not just those who hold positions of formal leadership in the church or organization but also those who lead by influence. It needs people who have both credibility and expertise. It requires those who can see the "big picture" to envision the dream of change as well as those who can decipher the details to manage the process of change.

It also must be said that certain people should not be included in a team charged with changing the status quo. It is best to avoid those who:

- Suffer from swollen egos—the task of driving change is bigger than the individual, and personal ambition needs to be sacrificed to the greater cause.

- Constantly make excuses—those who somehow never carry out what they promise quickly become part of the problem, not part of the solution.

- Run for the exit—disloyalty and a lack of commitment have no place.

A TASK THAT IS COMMUNICATED

Teams that create significant change are characterized by the honesty of their discussions, the quality of their relationships, and their willingness to invest time in each other. Those things cannot be achieved by rushed meetings at the end of the working day when everyone is tired and ready to go home. Team building requires whole days and even weekends spent together developing trust and defining the task. Good leaders give their best efforts and their quality time to focusing everyone and everything on the task ahead.

Directing Responsibility

Once the urgent need for change has been established, the importance of the work at hand communicated, and the team committed to the task, there needs to be an allocation of resources. It is crucial to realize that on a team whose mission is change, three distinct sets of responsibility are needed from visionaries, managers, and supervisors. To some extent, every team member should be able to share in these responsibilities as the need arises. However, individuals are usually more gifted in one area than in others. A team leader needs to identify the strengths of each member and structure the team using the best mix and balance.

> *Visionaries paint the pictures.* They are the ones who can see the desired future and hold up a vision that captivates the

imagination. They need to be set free to dream their dreams. In time, the vision is tested against hard reality, but without visionaries nothing ever changes.

Visionaries point to possibilities. They ask those teasing questions: "What if?" and "Why not?" They expand the boundaries and stretch the imagination. They force us to think outside the box. They provide incentive and inspiration for progress.

Managers provide the plans. They ask the hard questions: "Who will do it?" and "How and when will they do it?" Managers identify strategic thrusts and goals, draw up timetables, chart progress, and evaluate relative success or failure of the work. Without the discipline of managers, visionaries would be no more than daydreamers, and change would degenerate into wishful thinking.

Managers calculate the pennies. They do the unglamorous but essential task of working out the cost and deciding whether it is affordable. They draw up the financial projections and try to match the realities of existing resources to the possibilities of progress. Christian churches and organizations that neglect this aspect of managing change should not be viewed as deeply spiritual or as great examples of faith. They are merely irresponsible, and they run the risk of bringing their ministry into financial disaster and disrepute.

Supervisors drive the projects. They oversee practicalities. They are those indispensable individuals who accept the responsibility for seeing that plans are carried through and things actually get done. They are often underestimated, but wise leaders know just how much they are worth.

Supervisors direct the people. They encourage "buy in" at every level, extending and expanding the concept of "team" to include everyone in the organization. They are the equivalent of the factory foreman, the link between management and workers. Their more experienced insights can breathe reality into the vision and engender enthusiasm even in the most reluctant.

Only when visionaries, managers, and supervisors are working together is synergy released.

Demonstrating Bravery

Change is not for the faint-hearted. Leaders of change need to be giant slayers—and giants do not roll over easily! Here are two giants that must be overthrown if change is to take place and take hold:

UNCOOPERATIVE PEOPLE

Anyone who has ever tried to initiate change has faced the challenge of how to handle people in positions of responsibility who simply "dig in" and refuse to be cooperative. There are three simple rules for dealing with such individuals:

Always you must try to reach the person

Wise leaders avoid making snap judgments about difficult people. Instead, we take time to find out why a person is resistant to change. Is the problem simply that they don't understand? Is the call for change causing them to think that all they have done in the past is worthless? Are they feeling left out of the loop? Are they just slow starters who need time to get on board? If we want to show that change is imperative, we must learn what makes these people tick and how to make them feel important so that they will contribute to the change process, not deter it.

Often you must educate the person

When driving change, resistance often arises not from stubbornness but from feelings of inadequacy. People need to be equipped with new skills and trained in new practices, which incorporate the changes taking place around them. Transformation of an organization cannot take root without educating people.

Occasionally you must remove the person

I have a friend whose constant prayer, for himself and for others, is "Lord, change us or move us!" It is a prayer we all need to say, especially leaders of change. We must be brave enough to remove those who will not be reached and who refuse to learn in new directions. One of the most costly decisions leaders can make is to hold up progress—in line with God's will and for the common good—because of a reluctance to confront those who adamantly resist necessary change.

INHIBITING STRUCTURES

In addtion to overcoming the giant of uncooperative people, leaders also must face and defeat the giant of inhibiting structures for the cause of change. The challenge of this particular giant is that, like the Hydra in Greek mythology, it has more than one head!

Many churches and organizations have a style of government that is hierarchical and centralized, which worked reasonably well in a world where change was slow and life predictable. It is entirely unsuitable, however, in the postmodern world, where we need flexibility to respond to rapid shifts in culture. Leaders can bring about lasting and relevant change only if we are prepared to loosen our control, minimize the layers of administration, and delegate decision making to the point where we are connecting with the people we were called to serve.

In large denominations especially, a number of departments exist with different responsibilities related to the overall mission. All too often, there is a lack of synergy among them. Sometimes the problem is simply poor communication; at other times it is a matter of rivalry and struggle for control. If the matter is not confronted, however, all efforts at change will be thwarted as people dig in and try to defend their own kingdoms. Therefore, leaders need to ask: "Is this department really necessary? Is it contributing to the current mission? Can it be streamlined—or perhaps even eliminated—without adversely affecting the organization?"

Developing Tenacity

Leading change is not a short–term project. Only leaders and teams who develop tenacity will be able to see the process through to a successful conclusion. Once we have accepted the need for change, we are merely at the start of a long, tough journey.

ENSURING CONTINUITY

Change should have its own momentum. One change inevitably leads to another. In fact, some claim that in order to change one thing permanently, you end up having to change everything! To ensure that change is continuous and does not come grinding to a halt:

- The leader and the leadership team must not get bogged down in the details or in the mechanics of change. We must continue to give our best efforts to keeping the vision clear and focused.
- Communication and delegation must be the order of the day. Unless people continue to embrace the vision as their own and become part of the process, any changes will be shallow and short–lived.

TRANSFORMING CULTURE

There are those who claim that no changes can ever be made until the culture of a group is changed first. They are sadly mistaken! The *last* thing to change will be the culture of the group, and that will happen only after a long series of other successful and permanent changes. We first need to understand what "group culture" is and the twin pillars on which it is built.

Group culture arises largely from the ways in which people act, often without knowing it. They will tell you, "That's just the way we do things around here." People subscribe to behavioral norms without even realizing that it has happened, and promotion and preference tend to come to those who follow the unwritten codes. Those who don't follow are seen as "not our kind of people" and are often marginalized or excluded from the inner circles of the group.

More important, group culture is based on real, shared values of the group, which may, in truth, be very different from publicly stated aims. The mission statement of a church, for example, may announce that it exists to reach the lost, while the real passion of its members is, in fact, making music, enjoying each other's company, and maintaining their traditions. These cultural values are what really shape behavior, whatever the carefully prepared publicity may say. These values are what will stand the test of time—even when the membership changes.

Group culture is very difficult to challenge because it exerts its hold through the actions and attitudes of many individuals and because it is born and thrives on a subconscious level. The hard fact remains that culture will change only as people's behaviors change—and only when those changes produce positive results that are difficult to refute.

On the long, tough journey toward cultural transformation, tenacious leaders should demonstrate the following characteristics:

> *Courtesy*—Show proper respect for the old culture, recognizing what was good and acknowledging the faithfulness of good people who have served to the best of their ability.

> *Honesty*—Present the facts, nevertheless, that we live in a different time and the status quo is no longer an option. Encourage people to face these facts and no longer ignore the undeniable statistical trends.

> *Responsibility*—In the end, leadership means just what it says. Although a certain amount of delegation and consultation takes place, accept (even embrace!) responsibility for making the decisions that will expedite change.

Celebrating Victory

Lastly, leaders need to learn to celebrate each victory, the incremental markers of change. Good leaders are always optimistic and alert, and they know how to spot a significant victory:

- It's real—a genuine change for the good and for good.
- It's related to the primary mission.
- It's recognized by those affected as being an improvement.

They also know why it's worth celebrating that victory:

- It focuses on the evidence of change being for the better.
- It gives people working for change some encouragement.
- It adds to our expertise in the business of leading change.

And they know how to celebrate:

- A personal word of thanks to an individual who has gone the "extra mile" is always appreciated.

- A public acknowledgment of work well done (or successes gained) does much to raise the morale of the entire group.

- A party—anything from coffee and donuts at breaktime to an evening out for everyone—can go a long way toward healing the hurts and stresses along the bumpy road of change.

Good leaders know that only happy people can do the hard work that ongoing change requires. It is often said that everyone wants progress but no one likes change. It is a much more profound truth to say that the future belongs to those who can lead change in a manner that is both positive and palatable to as many as possible.

The Salvation Army in California had a simple slogan for its Christmas kettle campaign one year: "Change goes in, change comes out." The message was plain to all: If a whole lot of people give even a little, the effects in changed lives can be enormous. There is a parable here to encourage leaders in the church: If we motivate enough people to invest in a changing church, we may well see a world that is radically changed for the better. A transformed church might even be the instrument to bring about the answer to the greatest petition ever offered:

Thy kingdom come, Thy will be done, on earth as it is in heaven.

ten

Leading in a Crisis

For scientific leadership give me [Robert Falcon] Scott;
for swift and efficient travel, [Roald] Amundsen;
but when you are in a hopeless situation,
when there seems no way out,
get down on your knees and pray for Shackleton.

Alfred Lansing, Endurance: Shackleton's Incredible Voyage

The real test of any leader is how they handle a crisis. All leaders will have to face one sooner or later, and it will stretch them to the limit. It will test their nerves and challenge their abilities, but it will also be the place at which they learn most about themselves and the art of leadership. Of course, if a leader is wise, he or she will prepare for the inevitable by learning the basic tenets for dealing with a crisis.

Keep a Sense of Proportion

The problem with crises is that they appear to be so big that they tend to overwhelm us, but it's absolutely essential to anticipate this reaction and counteract it by heeding the following.

ACCEPT THAT CRISES WILL OCCUR

We live in a fallen world, where nothing is perfectly as God intended. People are frail and sinful and don't always behave as they should. Even leaders make mistakes at some point and consequently bring problems on themselves. For all these reasons, things just go wrong. As it is said about difficult times in life: "At times like these it's important to remember that there have always been times like these!"

ASK, IS THIS REALLY IMPORTANT?

When I started out in ministry I was, like other young leaders, full of enthusiasm and idealism. To be honest, I saw myself as something of a dragon slayer. I set out to solve every problem. At the first hint of any trouble, I was there with my lethal combination of strong discipline and conflict resolution. I soon realized, however, that I was actually creating problems, and I learned to stop and ask if each issue was really that important. By the time I had asked the question, half the problems had simply resolved themselves!

TAKE TIME TO THINK AND PRAY

Relatively few issues need to be solved this very minute. Wise leaders know that, despite the instinctive desire to move in swiftly, it is better to take a little time. Find out the facts, discuss the issues with trusted colleagues and more experienced leaders, and take time to lay the whole matter quietly before God. The wrong solution simply creates another problem, usually bigger than the first. A little thought, on the other hand, helps avoid a great deal of unnecessary pain.

KEEP A SENSE OF HUMOR

Some things are no joke, but a sense of humor serves as a tremendous relief in times of trouble. Leadership is a solemn business, but it can be and should be solemn fun. Even the most seemingly intractable problem will have a funny side. I have often seen the heat taken out of a confrontation by the careful use of humor. It can help angry people see how ridiculous they are being. It may not always solve the problem, but it usually dissolves the stress.

Keep to the Principles A through E

Admit mistakes you have made

A willingness to apologize is a key weapon in the armory of a leader. When problems arise because of our own mistakes, we need to admit it, ask all concerned for their forgiveness, and learn from the experience. A youth worker once introduced his new assistant by joking, "All the people we wanted turned us down, so we had to choose Mary." Of course, he was only kidding, but the joke misfired and Mary was offended. When she expressed her feelings, he immediately went on the attack: "Surely you can take a joke," he responded. Sadly, the relationship never recovered. If he had made a simple apology, the outcome would have been different.

Bring out any honest disagreements

Whenever a conflict flares up, we often tend to smooth things down, to insist that everything is fine and that everyone is happy. But this kind of placating only exacerbates a difficult situation. People end up feeling frustrated and angry, and those feelings spill over into further clashes between individuals or groups. Instead, leaders must learn to allow honest disagreements to surface and then give opportunity for feelings to be expressed. Depending on the situation, a leader may bring the warring parties together or meet them separately, allowing them to have their say in a safe environment. However it is done, this part of the process of conflict resolution cannot be avoided.

Confront people who are deliberately disruptive

Disputes mostly occur because of differing viewpoints. By addressing the issues and allowing people to have their say, the majority of confrontations can be avoided. However, there are also occasions when it becomes clear that someone is being deliberately disruptive. In these cases, avoiding confrontation would be a failure of leadership. Such moments are never easy, but difficult people must realize that their conduct cannot be allowed to continue unchallenged. That's when a leader needs to demonstrate a combination of courtesy and firmness, resisting the temptation to become embroiled in an argument, respecting the dignity of the offender, but resolutely insisting on a change of conduct or attitude.

DEMONSTRATE POSITIVE ATTITUDES AND HEALTHY PROCESSES

Times of crisis provide unequaled opportunities for leaders to demonstrate how relationships should be conducted, especially when things are difficult. Leaders can show how it is possible to disagree without being disagreeable: Each person concerned must be given the opportunity to speak without being interrupted or shouted down, every side of the problem must be examined, and decisions must be explained. Sulking or seeking revenge is not acceptable. When positive examples are set forth, people begin to appreciate that what matters is not the difficulty itself, but how it is handled; and leaders start to understand that tensions—far from being destructive—can be used productively to increase a team's growth and maturity.

EXPLORE THE OPTIONS

What follows are five approaches to solving a crisis or conflict. Each varies in its intent or desired outcome; some focus more on what is achieved, others on how relationships are affected.

Withdraw

Condition: Tempers are flaring and feelings are so high that things are best left for the moment.

Outcome: Little will be achieved, and relationships will not ultimately be strengthened.

Yield

Condition: Some things may be causing dissent, but one party may decide that, given the cost in emotional energy, it is best simply to allow the other person to have their way.

Outcome: Relationships will be preserved, but the situation will not change.

Compromise
> *Condition:* There is no principle at stake.

> *Outcome:* It is a valid solution, a good short–term answer that allows time for tempers to cool and further thought to take place. The danger is that no one is entirely satisified.

Win
> *Condition:* When dealing with a deliberately disruptive person, it is sometimes the only way to go.

> *Outcome:* It may achieve the aim, but it does nothing for relationships.

Resolve
> *Condition:* Whenever there is an opportunity to think creatively and ask, Is there a better way of doing things that we haven't thought of? How can everyone find something to gain from the situation?

> *Outcome:* This approach can achieve the right end and enhance relationships.

Keep Your Poise

Facing a difficult challenge can push any leader into extremes of attitude and behavior. Anyone who has negotiated his or her way through a crisis knows how easily it can upset our physical, spiritual, and emotional balance. So here are some hints for keeping your poise in the uneven terrain of conflict, confusion, and complexity.

SPEAKING OF PAIN

Leaders don't like to admit we've been hurt. In the middle of a crisis, you will hear us say, "I'm fine, no problems." It is far healthier, instead, to admit our frailty and acknowledge our hurt. Otherwise, we may pay the price—often months after the crisis is over—in emotional, spiritual, moral, or family breakdown.

HOLDING A HAND WHILE STANDING ALONE

We all know that leaders sometimes have to stand alone and face criticism to which they cannot reply without betraying confidences. That is part of the role of a leader, but it is a dangerous place to stand. Those who stay there too long lose all sense of perspective and begin to develop a martyr complex. To prevent this, try finding a mentor or counselor—a trustworthy, reliable source with whom to confide the pain and receive guidance (see chapter five: The Consistent Leader).

TIMING IS EVERYTHING

Procrastination is the enemy of crisis resolution. A man's gotta do what a man's gotta do! And he better do it without delay. On the other hand, to rush in where angels fear to tread is equally dangerous. If timing is the essence of good comedy, it is equally important to the exercise of authority. Remember: *Take time to think and pray.*

GENERALLY SPEAKING IN TOO MUCH DETAIL

A mistake that leaders make when handling a crisis is a leaning on generalities when searching for solutions. The words "always" and "never" should be avoided. Language needs to be specific and precise with regard to each incident. At the same time, we need to be aware of the danger of citing every detail involved in the conflict, particularly when disciplining an individual. The purpose is to reach a resolution, not to beat someone into submission!

NOT RUTHLESS, BUT NOT TOOTHLESS

An experienced leader once gave me a piece of excellent advice: "Never take a man to pieces in such a way that you cannot put him together again before he leaves your office." We need to be honest with people, but not so ruthless as to be ultimately destructive. Remember that we are in the business of restoration.

The opposite danger to being ruthless is being toothless! I have been in disciplinary hearings where proper discipline was replaced by a warm, fuzzy pseudo–compassion, which almost amounted to a pat on the back for the offender and left everyone wondering just who was at fault. Leaders need to be brave enough to administer a rebuke yet loving enough to offer a road back.

WHEN PRIVACY BECOMES A LIABILITY

Rebuke is better done in private, but when confronting the opposite sex, it is unwise to be alone with the person. Words can be misconstrued and misquoted, actions can be misunderstood. It is best to have someone else present as a witness and, when appropriate, encourage the person who must be confronted to bring someone with them.

Both as a useful learning tool and as a record of events, it is also wise to keep written notes of meetings and a journal of your handling of any crisis situation.

Keep Your Personality

Much more could be said on the subject of leadership, but that is for other writers and other books. One final word: Learn all you can from every leader you know. Ask every question you can think of from those you admire and trust. Listen to the wise counsel of those who are your leaders and those whom you have the privilege to lead. But never forget that God made you. Your strengths and weaknesses, your gifts and abilities, your entire personality—they are all the equipment you need, when refined by grace and honed by study and application, to be the leader God wants you to be. Be yourself, be your best self, and watch what God can do in and with and through you.

The Mission Statement
of The Salvation Army USA

The Salvation army, an international movement, is an evangelical part of the universal Christian Church. Its message is based on the Bible. Its ministry is motivated by the love of God. Its mission is to preach the gospel of Jesus Christ and to meet human needs in His name without discrimination.

CREST BOOKS

Salvation Army National Publications

Crest Books, a division of The Salvation Army's National Publications department, was established in 1997 so contemporary Salvationist voices could be captured and bound in enduring form for future generations, to serve as witnesses to the continuing force and mission of the Army.

Never the Same Again
BY SHAW CLIFTON

Christians are sometimes overwhelmed by what they feel are confusing explanations of the deeper aspects of faith. The author makes these readily understandable by drawing on his thorough knowledge of Scripture to help seekers establish a sure foundation. Clifton encourages new believers' enthusiasm for Christ while guiding them through roadblocks that can stunt spiritual growth. He addresses such questions as: Can I be sure I'm saved? How much like Jesus can I be? Will God equip me to serve Him? An ideal resource for seekers and new converts, individuals making recommitments, and leaders of discipling groups.

Celebrate the Feasts of the Lord
BY WILLIAM W. FRANCIS

Author William Francis presents an examination of the feasts and fasts established by God in Leviticus 23, as well as those inaugurated after the Babylonian exile. With studied skill, he examines the historical background of each feast and makes clear its significance for the modern Christian. This book meets a critical need by revealing how Jesus participated in the feasts during His earthly life and how, in Himself, their meaning was fulfilled. Study guides follow each chapter, allowing readers to explore and apply new insights, making this book ideal for groups.

Christmas Through the Years:
A War Cry *Treasury*

Through the years, the pages of the Christmas *War Cry* have proclaimed the timeless message of the birth of the Babe of Bethlehem. *Christmas Through the Years* contains articles, stories, poetry, and art that have inspired readers over the past half century. This treasury highlights Salvationists of wide appeal from General Evangeline Booth (1948) to General John Gowans and also features contributors such as Billy Graham and Joni Eareckson Tada.

Easter Through the Years:
A War Cry Treasury

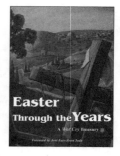

A companion volume to *Christmas Through the Years*, this treasury of work culled from the Easter *War Cry* over the last 50 years recounts the passion of Christ and unpacks the events surrounding the cross and the numerous ways Easter intersects with life and faith today. Contributors include Joni Eareckson Tada, Max Lucado, Commissioner Samuel Logan Brengle and General William Booth.

Who Are These Salvationists?
BY SHAW CLIFTON

Clifton has written a seminal study exploring the Army's roots, theology, and position in the body of believers while providing readers with a definitive profile of Salvationism. The book is intended to help Salvationists understand their historical and theological roots as it shapes their ideas of the Army's mission in the new century. In addition, Clifton has succeeded in providing non–Salvationists with the most comprehensive portrait of the Army and its soldiers thus far, introducing them to the theology driving our social action.

Pictures from the Word
BY MARLENE CHASE

"The Bible is full of beautiful word pictures, concrete images that bring to life spiritual ideas," writes Chase. "God's personality is poignantly revealed to us in such images as a hen sheltering her chicks or a loving Father engraving the names of His children into His hands. These and a host of other images teach us about God and about ourselves." In 56 meditations, the author brings vivid metaphors of Scripture to life, illuminating familiar passages and addressing frequent references to the vulnerability of man met by God's limitless and gracious provision.

A Little Greatness
BY JOE NOLAND

Under the expert tutelage of author Joe Noland, readers explore the book of Acts, revealing the paradoxes of the life of a believer. Using word play and alliteration, Noland draws us into the story of the early Church while demonstrating the contemporary relevance of all that took place. The book is divided into three parts, which address shared aspects of heavenly greatness available through the help of the Holy Spirit: great power, great grace, and great joy. A Bible study and discussion guide for each chapter helps the reader apply each lesson, making this an ideal group study resource.

Fractured Parables
BY A. KENNETH WILSON

By applying truths of Scripture to contemporary situations, we find that people of the Bible are as real as we are today. Wilson helps readers view beloved biblical accounts in a new light by recasting Jesus' parables in modern circumstances and language. His knack for finding humor in the mundane and gems of truth in earthly guise will lighten hearts and quicken spirits.

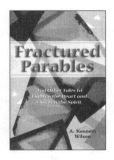

Slightly Off Center!
Growth Principles to Thaw Frozen Paradigms
BY TERRY CAMSEY

An expert in the field of church health, Camsey seeks to thaw frozen paradigms of what is "Army." He challenges us to see things from a different perspective and urges us to welcome a new generation of Salvationists whose methods may be different but whose hearts are wholly God's—and whose mission remains consistent with the fundamental principles William Booth established.

He Who Laughed First:
Delighting in a Holy God
BY PHIL NEEDHAM

Needham questions why there are so many sour–faced saints when the Christian life is meant to be joyful. In his book he explores the secret to enduring joy, a joy that is not found by following some list of prescriptions, but by letting God make us holy, by letting Him free us to become who we are in Christ—saints. *He Who Laughed First* helps us discover the why and how of becoming a joyful, hilarious saint.

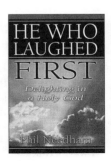

Romance & Dynamite:
Essays on Science and the Nature of Faith
BY LYELL M. RADER

"Whatever God makes works, and works to perfection. So does His plan for turning life from a rat race to a rapture." Anecdotes and insights on the interplay of science and faith are found in this collection of essays by one of the Army's most indefatigable evangelists. As a Salvation Army officer, Rader used his training as a chemist to prove the trustworthiness of the Bible, find evidence of the Creator's hand in everything, and demonstrate why the saving knowledge of God is crucial to understanding life's value and purpose.

A Salvationist Treasury
EDITED BY HENRY GARIEPY

This book brings to readers the quintessence of devotional writings from Salvationist authors spanning over 100 years. From Army notables to the virtually unknown, from the classics to the contemporary, this treasure trove of 365 inspirational readings will enrich your life, deepen your devotional study and enhance your grasp of the Army's principles and mission. *A Salvationist Treasury* is certain to become a milestone compilation of Army literature.

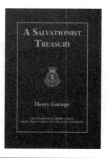

Our God Comes:
And Will Not Be Silent
BY MARLENE CHASE

Our God Comes rests on the premise that, like the unstoppable ocean tide, God comes to us in a variety of ways and His voice will not be silent as He reveals Himself throughout all Creation. This book of poetry, the first of its kind for Crest Books, invites the reader to contemplate life's experiences and God's goodness to us. An accomplished writer and poet, Chase offers a book that lends itself to devotional meditation, small group discussion, and the literary enjoyment of carefully crafted poetry.

If Two Shall Agree
BY CARROLL FERGUSON HUNT

The book is a fascinating story of how God brought Paul and Kay Rader together and melded them into a team who served in The Salvation Army for over 35 years. Readers will follow on the journey from General Rader's memories of his parents' innovative ministry in New York to his election to the highest office in the Army and then as president of Asbury College. Combined with the vision of his wife Kay for greater ministry of women in the Army, readers will see the power and far-reaching influence in this couple, who serve together as one in the name of Christ.

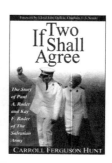

Pen of Flame:
The Life and Poetry of Catherine Baird
BY JOHN C. IZZARD

Catherine Baird lived a life of extraordinary artistic value to The Salvation Army. As a poet, hymn writer, and editor, Baird changed the way the Army viewed the importance of the written word. From a decade of research and devotion John C. Izzard has painted a compelling word picture of one of the Army's strongest and yet most delicate authors.

Andy Miller:
A Legend and a Legacy
BY HENRY GARIEPY

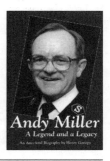

This biography by Colonel Henry Gariepy seeks, through anecdotes, to convey the story of one of the most colorful and remarkable leaders in the history of The Salvation Army. As an American Salvationist, Andy Miller has had a powerful spiritual impact on countless numbers, both within and outside the ranks of the Army. His vast ministry across the nation has left its indelible mark on innumerable lives.

A Word in Season:
A collection of short stories

All having appeared in *The War Cry*, these stories journey through the seasons and around the world, taking readers on the ups and downs of everyday existence—made extraordinary through faith. Described as "chicken soup with a dash of Salvationism," *A Word in Season* features factual accounts of historic events as well as fictional narratives. Over 30 authors, including Max Lucado, have contributed to this thoughtful compilation of the joys and sadnesses of life within the panoply of Christian belief.

Sanctified Sanity:
The Life and Teaching of Samuel Logan Brengle
BY R. DAVID RIGHTMIRE

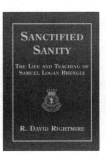

Rightmire, Professor of Bible and Theology at Asbury College in Wilmore, Kentucky, has written a theological reassessment of Samuel Logan Brengle's life and thought to reacquaint those of the Wesleyan–holiness tradition in general, and the Army in particular, with the legacy of this holiness apostle. With this significant work, the author aims to make Brengle's many theological pronouncements on holiness accessible to those who are unfamiliar with his teachings. Emphasis is placed on Brengle's understanding of the work of the Holy Spirit in sanctification, which is the focus of his preaching and literary contributions.

All of the titles listed above can be purchased through your nearest Salvation Army Supplies and Purchasing department:

ATLANTA, GA—(800) 786–7372

DES PLAINES, IL—(847) 294–2012

RANCHO PALOS VERDES, CA—(800) 937–8896

WEST NYACK, NY—(888) 488–4882